Rüdiger Liedtke | Laszlo Trankovits

111 Places in Cape Town That You Must Not Miss

emons:

© Emons Verlag GmbH
All rights reserved
Design: Eva Kraskes, based on a design
by Lübbeke | Naumann | Thoben
Maps: altancicek.design, www.altancicek.de
English translation: Dr. Fredric Kroll
Printing and binding: Grafisches Centrum Cuno, Calbe
Printed in Germany 2015
First edition

Did you enjoy it? Do you want more?
Join us in uncovering new places around the world on:
www.111places.com

Foreword

Do you know where precious gems slumber in Cape Town? Or where you can sample 500 types of whiskey along the water's edge – or meet a penguin while bathing?

With far more than a million tourists a year, Cape Town is among the world's most attractive destinations. Named by the *New York Times* as the number one place to go in 2014, this modern and creative metropolis at the base of Table Mountain, with its turbulent history of colonialism, apartheid, and liberation, is as culturally complex and fascinating, as it is disarmingly beautiful. Here is where the European settlement of South Africa began – with all its conflicts. Here, at the apex of segregation, the whites forcibly displaced the population of an entire district and then leveled it to the ground – but it was also here that Nelson Mandela, after his release, proclaimed the new South Africa. And it was here, too, that Desmond Tutu, the former Archbishop of Cape Town, envisioned the "rainbow nation": a country in which all races and ethnicities would live together in peace.

But did you know, that even today, there is only one vineyard in the Cape region wholly owned by black South Africans? Or that you can come face to face with four Nobel Peace Prize winners right in the middle of the city? And that the area not only sports endlessly long beaches and breathtaking landscapes, but that there is also a lively theatre and jazz scene, and that medical history was made here, many years ago?

Cape Town is one of the most beautiful places on earth – and offers many surprises above and beyond the usual sights. *111 Places in Cape Town That You Must Not Miss* presents this exciting city and its environs from an insider's point of view.

111 Places

1___ The African Music Store
A continent presents itself in a record shop | 10

2___ aMadoda Braii
A hint of the townships in Woodstock | 12

3___ The Arthouse Cinema
Cape Town's oldest movie theater is still alive | 14

4___ The Assembly Room
Big stage of a tumultuous history | 16

5___ The Aquarium
Underwater worlds on the waterfront | 18

6___ The Auwal Mosque
The oldest Muslim house of worship | 20

7___ The Bascule Bar
Where whiskey is like wine | 22

8___ The Baxter
Cape Town's most versatile stage | 24

9___ Bay Harbour Market
A market that likes to celebrate | 26

10___ The Beach Cabins
Newfound symbols of freedom | 28

11___ The Bird Clinic
A bird in need is a friend indeed | 30

12___ Bloubergstrand Beach
Sunset in front of Table Mountain | 32

13___ Bo-Kaap
Cape Town's vibrant district | 34

14___ The Book Lounge
Read and let read | 36

15___ The Campus
A university rich in treasures | 38

16___ Canal Walk
South Africa's biggest shopping center | 40

17___ The Cape
A visit to the Cape of Good Hope | 42

18___ The Cape Houses
Historic architecture on the Cape | 44

19 — Cape to Cuba
In homage to Che Guevara | 46

20 — The Castle
A sense of colonial times in the Castle of Good Hope | 48

21 — Chapman's Peak Drive
A toll well spent | 50

22 — The Clock Tower
Former residence of the Port Captain | 52

23 — The Colonial Houses
Strolling along the Historic Mile | 54

24 — The Colonial Monument
Where Vasco da Gama is commemorated | 56

25 — The Crypt
Jazz beneath Desmond Tutu's church | 58

26 — De Waal Park
Green oasis below Molteno Reservoir | 60

27 — De Waterkant
Free to be you and me | 62

28 — The Design Centre
Watch artists at work in Montebello | 64

29 — The Diamond House
A precious history presented in a precious home | 66

30 — The Disa Park Towers
Where perspectives collide | 68

31 — The District Six Museum
A sinister chapter of apartheid | 70

32 — Evita se Perron
A theater for Pieter-Dirk Uys | 72

33 — The Flea Market
Bargains galore in Milnerton | 74

34 — The Flower Market
Fresh blooms for more than a century | 76

35 — The Flying Archbishop
God bless your lunch | 78

36 — The Freemason Temple
Architectural jewel behind Parliament | 80

37 — The Fugard Theatre
Modern stage against racism | 82

38 — The Gallery Crawl
Treasure trove for art lovers | 84

39__ The Gandhi Monument
Meet the great Indian leader at the University | 86

40__ The Grand Café
Relaxing on the beach | 88

41__ The Grand Daddy
Spend the night on the roof | 90

42__ The GrandWest Casino
The palace of diversions | 92

43__ The Gravestone
The garden of extinct plants | 94

44__ Heritage Square
A block full of surprises | 96

45__ The Imhoff Farm
Three dozen stores under one roof | 98

46__ The Irma Stern Museum
The great artist's eccentric lifestyle | 100

47__ The Khayelitsha Shopping Center
Shopping in the Cape Flats | 102

48__ The Labour Museum
The history of revolts and strikes | 104

49__ Langa Cultural Center
Art and music in the township | 106

50__ The Leopard
How the big cat got on the rock | 108

51__ The Lighthouse
The seamark at Green Point | 110

52__ The Lion Compound
Wild animals in Vredenheim | 112

53__ The Marble Staircase
Where the end of apartheid began | 114

54__ The Maritime Centre
Noteworthy information on South-African seafaring | 116

55__ M'hudi
The first black-owned wine vineyard in South Africa | 118

56__ The Motor Museum
Old-timers in the midst of the Winelands | 120

57__ The Motorcycle Joint
Drive right up to the counter | 122

58__ Muizenberg Station
A detour on the way to Simon's Town | 124

59 | The Mutual Building
Africa's first highrise | 126

60 | Mzoli's
Braii at the butcher of Gugulethu | 128

61 | The National Library
Chilling out in the historic reading room | 130

62 | Nobel Square
South Africa's four Nobel Peace Prize winners | 132

63 | The Noon Gun
Shooting off at midday since 1806 | 134

64 | The Oasis
Settling down in Company's Garden | 136

65 | The Observatory
Reaching for the stars under Cape Town's skies | 138

66 | The Old Biscuit Mill
Woodstock's "insider" Saturday market | 140

67 | The Operating Room
Where Professor Barnard transplanted his first heart | 142

68 | The Organ
Listening to the old masters in Groote Kerk | 144

69 | The Ostrich Farm
Meet gigantic birds in the national park | 146

70 | Oude Bank Bakkerij
Considered the best bakery on the Cape | 148

71 | Panama Jacks
Offbeat fish restaurant hidden in the harbor | 150

72 | Panorama Highway
Where you meet wild baboons | 152

73 | Peers Cave
Traces of human life in the Stone Age | 154

74 | The Penguin Colony
Witness a miracle of nature in Boulders | 156

75 | The Plateau
Having a good time on Table Mountain | 158

76 | Pollsmoor Prison
Lunch in Mandela's prison | 160

77 | The Quarry
Forced labor on Robben Island | 162

78 | The Racetrack
Betting on horses at the city gates | 164

79___ The Revolver
Memorial against violence | 166

80___ The Rhodes Memorial
Resting at the political visionary's feet | 168

81___ The Rugby Museum
Where the Springboks are revered | 170

82___ Rust en Vreugd
18th-century Cape architecture | 172

83___ The Saltwater Pool
Relaxed swimming near the breakwater | 174

84___ The San Centre
The bush people's old country | 176

85___ The Seven Memorial
Commemorating the victims of state terror | 178

86___ The Shark Monument
Mobile high-tech sculpture | 180

87___ Signal Hill
Flying high above the city | 182

88___ The "Ski Jump"
Expressway to nowhere | 184

89___ Slangkop Point
The tallest cast-iron lighthouse on the Cape | 186

90___ The Slave Church
Where slaves were forced to become Christians | 188

91___ South Africa's Hollywood
A hotbed for filmmaking | 190

92___ The Souvenir Garden
Life-sized mementos | 192

93___ Straight No Chaser
Feel the beat of Cape Town's jazz scene | 194

94___ The Synagogue
Jewish life on the Cape | 196

95___ The Taal Monument
Monument to the Afrikaans language | 198

96___ The Test Kitchen
A little restaurant with a great reputation | 200

97___ The Theatre on the Bay
Where the avant-garde crowds together | 202

98___ The Toboggan Park
Downhill thrills for all ages | 204

99___ The Treadmill
Instrument of torture at Breakwater Lodge | 206

100___ The Tree Walkway
Tiptoeing through the treetops | 208

101___ The Turkish Bath
100 years of aquatic joy | 210

102___ The Underground Tunnels
Mysterious downtown underworld | 212

103___ Vergelegen Wine Farm
The wine farm and slavery | 214

104___ Waterkloof
The restaurant in a giant glass cube | 216

105___ The White Circle
The center of the city | 218

106___ Wilderer Distillery
The masters of grappa | 220

107___ The Wildlife Reservation
Africa's fauna not far from Cape Town | 222

108___ The Wine Route
Wine farms behind Table Mountain | 224

109___ The Wine Tram
A historic tram ride through the wine region | 226

110___ The World Championship Stadium
The UFO that landed in Green Point | 228

111___ The Zip Zap
Integration in a playful way | 230

1 The African Music Store
A continent presents itself in a record shop

The African Music Store has been a beloved fixture on Long Street since 1997, when owner Mark Charnas and his partners first opened the shop. Stocking Cape Town's widest range of African CDs from all over the continent, it's the go-to source for domestic music of every kind. The sound of African rhythms can already be heard from the sidewalk as one approaches the store. Once inside, it's so loud that you have to get right next to the ear of one of the extremely competent and knowledgeable salespersons to ask for what you want. But you can also browse among the numerous shelves and sample CDs at one of the listening stations as long as you like without being pressured to buy anything.

Visitors get a perfect overview of the variety of African music styles – from Cape Town jazz to gospel, classical, soul, house, dance, hip-hop, and, of course, kwaito, a type of local urban music that was born in the townships and spread throughout the city. The Afro-Cuban department and the huge assortment of reggae records are also highly recommendable. If you hear music anywhere in South Africa that you want to take home with you, you'll very likely find it here. In fact, there is a section of the store devoted purely to independent local artists. In addition to CDs and DVDs, the colorful shop also offers souvenirs and gifts – from exotic clothing and fun printed T-shirts to a range of African musical instruments.

Live music is very popular in Cape Town, and the city has an ebulliently creative club and jazz scene. Contributing to this are the many South-African jazz greats who lived in exile during apartheid, but have since returned and now perform regularly – such as the splendid jazz musician Abdullah Ibrahim, who lives in Cape Town and founded M7, an academy to train young South-African musicians.

Address 134 Long Street, City, Cape Town 8001, Tel +27/214260857, www.africanmusicstore.co.za | **Getting there** By public transit: Bus 101, Longmarket stop; "Hop on-Hop off" bus, Long Street stop | **Hours** Mon–Fri 9am–6pm, Sat 9am–2pm | **Tip** Live music is played on Long Street in Kennedy's cigar lounge and restaurant (No. 251) and Mama Africa (No. 178). You can book music tours of the city's clubs, such as the Cape Town Jazz Safari or the Cape Town Reggae Route (organizer: Coffeebeans Routes, www.coffeebeansroutes.com).

2 aMadoda Braii
A hint of the townships in Woodstock

This rather strident joint harks back to a time when such places were politically significant in South Africa's major cities. aMadoda didn't open until 2007, but it keeps the memory of the country's stormy history alive.

Located in the remotest corner of Woodstock, aMadoda is not a typical tourist destination. Reggae, hip-hop, and electro boom out of the loudspeakers of this fantastically painted restaurant with its old jukebox and billiard tables. Its *braai* (Afrikaans for "grill") specialties are meant to be eaten with your bare hands. There aren't any waiters. The website sums it up: "Whether you want to dance, chill, party, groove, laugh, chat, relax, unwind or have a feast, aMadoda is de place to be!"

Bringing a whiff of the townships into an area formerly inhabited almost exclusively by whites was this eatery's original concept. During apartheid, there were many forbidden or unlicensed joints on the outskirts of Cape Town – clandestine rendezvous for black workers and students as well as white opponents of apartheid. In such establishments as the legendary Don Pedro's, literary readings and political meetings were held – but there were also parties with dancing and music.

Close by, at aMadoda, you can still sense the rebellious atmosphere. Young African avant-garde jazz players or kwaito musicians often perform here, and you'll see leaflets everywhere.

It's quite evident that very political owners are behind this place. In the Xhosa language, *amadoda* means "men" – ostensibly the only word in this language in which the English syllable "mad" can be found, apart from *Madiba*, the name of Nelson Mandela's clan. The company backing aMadoda thus calls itself Mad World.

Address 1–4 Strand Street, Woodstock, Cape Town 7915, Tel +27/214472133, www.amadoda.co.za | **Getting there** By car: from downtown, take Newmarket Street (R 102) into Albert Road, turn left onto Railway Street and take first left onto Strand Street. By public transit: Bus 102, Kent Street stop or Woodstock Station, and then around 10 minutes on foot | **Hours** Mon–Thurs 12–9pm, Fri–Sun 12pm–2am | **Tip** Ashanti Design, 133–135 Sir Lowry Road, is a store with African handicrafts and unusual souvenirs.

3 The Arthouse Cinema
Cape Town's oldest movie theater is still alive

Looking back on a 65-year history, the Labia is the oldest movie theater in Cape Town – and also one of the most beautiful. In the 1940s, the house in the Gardens District was a ballroom for the nearby Italian embassy; in 1949, it was turned into a theater and cabaret. It was converted into a movie theater in the mid-1970s, so that it now has about a 40-year-long cinematic past.

In 1989, lawyer Ludi Kraus from Namibia took over the aging and correspondingly run-down Labia and renovated it, without substantially altering its character. He thus established the country's oldest independent artistic cinema.

During his initial years, Kraus was in constant conflict with the apartheid regime's censorship regulations; after 1994, he was able to screen whatever movies he wanted. Today, the Labia is a showcase for both challenging and amusing arthouse films.

The house has a total of 400 seats divided across four halls, of which the traditional one with 176 seats is the biggest. The chairs are still the originals, although with new and comfortable upholstery. Lots of things in the Labia are just like they used to be. The wooden ticket cabin in the cozy foyer with its red armchairs and sofas is from its early period as a theater, as are the small snack bar and the outdoor terrace.

You can take your glass of wine or beer with you into the movie hall. As most of the audience is demanding, high-quality films are shown, including many European productions – without completely renouncing Hollywood blockbusters. The focus of the program, however, is outside the mainstream. In cooperation with several neighboring restaurants, two tickets to the Labia are included with a good meal several days a week.

Address The Labia Theatre, 68 Orange Street, Gardens, Cape Town 8000, Tel +27/214245927, www.thelabia.co.za | **Getting there** By public transit: Bus 101, Government Avenue stop; "Hop on-Hop off" bus, Mount Nelson Hotel stop | **Hours** See newspaper and Internet listings for movie times | **Tip** Very close by stands the Mount Nelson Hotel, with its splendid garden and terrace, where it is particularly pleasant to have a drink in the late afternoon.

4   The Assembly Room
Big stage of a tumultuous history

The division of powers can be visualized geographically in South Africa. Since 2010, Cape Town has been the seat of the South African Parliament, while executive business is carried out in Pretoria. Since 1997, the judiciary, with the Supreme Court, has resided in Bloemfontain.

The Parliament building, constructed in 1884 in Georgian and Victorian style with Corinthian colonnades, was expanded repeatedly over the years and now comprises a gigantic complex between Parliament Street and Company's Garden. Until 2004, it was only a seasonal representation of the people, with lawmakers moving cumbersomely back and forth between Pretoria in the winter and Cape Town in the summer. Today, Parliament meets in the historic assembly room year-round; the parliamentary session is ceremoniously opened in January or February – an event that regularly brings Cape Town's inner city to a standstill. The Parliament building's lush garden is crowned by a statue of Queen Victoria, who reigned from 1837 to 1901.

The assembly room symbolizes South Africa's stormy and dramatic history. It was here that most of the severest laws of apartheid were passed, and that parliamentary legitimacy, ruled by the whites, was given to the regime. It was also here that one of the ideologists of apartheid, former Prime Minister Hendrik Verwoerd, was knifed to death by a parliamentary messenger of mixed racial descent. In 1994, Nelson Mandela gave his first great speech as president in the assembly room – which marked the official end of apartheid and South Africa's transition to a parliamentary system of government, as well as the implementation of equal rights for all cultures, sexes, and skin colors. You can visit the building and witness parliamentary debates from the public gallery.

Address 90 Plein Street, City, Cape Town 8001, Tel +27/214032266, www.parliament.gov.za | **Getting there** By public transit: Bus 103, Roeland Street stop, or bus 102/103, Darling Street stop; "Hop on-Hop off" bus, St. George's Cathedral stop | **Hours** 9am–4pm, guided tours: Mon–Fri 9am, 10am, 11am and noon; reservations required | **Tip** The nearby Tuynhuys, built in the 17th century, is the president's representative seat during sojourns in Cape Town.

5_ The Aquarium
Underwater worlds on the waterfront

South Africa – the country where the cool Atlantic and the warmer Indian Ocean meet at its southernmost point – has the only aquarium of its kind in the world. Opened in 1995, the Two Oceans Aquarium presents the fascinating denizens of both bodies of water. In 30-some pools encompassing an area of more than an acre, visitors can observe upwards of 300 species of water-loving creatures, including sharks, sea horses, reptiles, giant tortoises, sea lions, and penguins.

You can immerse yourself in this underwater realm from a variety of perspectives. In the Kelp Forest, for example, the sub-aquatic world is presented just as it is on the actual ocean floor, where kelp plants can grow as tall as trees. Also particularly impressive is the Predator Exhibit, which is housed in a two-story-high basin with a capacity of 2 million liters protected by a layer of acrylic glass a foot thick. Here, you can meet gigantic stingrays and numerous sand tiger sharks face-to-face. Although rather terrifying in appearance, this species of shark is actually considered quite docile unless provoked.

Those with a diving license and the appropriate experience can dive in the exhibit with trained guides. Novices can even register for a one-day crash course to get a dive certification. But all that most visitors want is to watch these carnivores, with their sharp rows of teeth, receive their daily feedings.

The Two Oceans Aquarium is located in the Victoria & Albert Waterfront, which opened in 1991 and was sold for 1.3 billion euros to a British-Arabian consortium in 2006. In 2012, however, South African investment company Growthpoint Properties Ltd. and the Public Investment Corporation (PIC) bought the Waterfront back. They now plan to expand the area all the way to Green Point.

Address Two Oceans Aquarium, Dock Road, V&A Waterfront, Cape Town 8002, Tel +27/214183823, www.aquarium.co.za | **Getting there** By public transit: Bus 104, Aquarium stop; "Hop on-Hop off" bus, Aquarium stop | **Hours** Daily 9.30am–6pm, Dec and Jan until 7pm | **Tip** A ride on the nearby Ferris wheel offers a completely different view of the V&A Waterfront and the harbor.

6 — The Auwal Mosque
The oldest Muslim house of worship

South Africa's oldest mosque calls itself "a symbol of the struggle of the Cape's Muslims for their freedom and the acknowledgment of Islam."

The Auwal Mosque was constructed in 1798 on a plot belonging to Coridon van Ceylon – a freed slave who was the very first Cape Malay to own land. As most of the Cape's Muslims, he came from Southeast Asia, where the colonial lords once kidnapped slaves in order to relieve a shortage of labor. Long years passed before the muezzin was permitted to call for prayers from the building originally conceived as a warehouse, as the dominant Dutch Reformed Church had no tolerance for other – especially non-Christian – religions.

The mosque is situated in the middle of picturesque and dynamic Bo-Kaap (also known as the Malay Quarter), whose rainbow-colored houses and cobblestone streets lie on the east side of Signal Hill. Despite the immigration of a diverse mixture of peoples, this district is dominated by Muslims. Though historically home to a Jewish population as well, there have been very few conflicts between these two groups throughout the centuries that they have lived together here.

Today, eleven mosques are located in Bo-Kaap and the nearby city center. The biggest one, its tall minaret visible from afar, is the Jamia Mosque, at the corner of Chiappini and Castle Streets. Built in 1850, it was the first Muslim house of worship permitted by British colonialists, and for this reason has the second name Queen Victoria Mosque. Some of the other Muslim houses of worship hardly differ from the private residences around them – the Palm Tree Mosque, on Long Street, for example.

The Auwal Mosque was reconstructed after the building collapsed in 1930. Only two of the original walls remain.

Address 39 Dorp Street, Bo-Kaap, Cape Town 8001, www.auwalmasjid.co.za | **Getting there** By public transit: Bus 101, Church oder Leeuwen Street stop; "Hop on-Hop off" bus, Jewel Africa stop | **Hours** Daily 10am–5pm; one-hour services are at 1pm, 3:30pm, and 6pm | **Tip** A paradise for cooks, the Atlas Trading Company, which specializes in Indian spices and products, can be found at 94 Wale Street.

7_ The Bascule Bar
Where whiskey is like wine

There are a number of attractive bars around the Victoria and Albert Waterfront – but none that offer such a unique wealth of whiskeys from all over the world as the Bascule Bar in the Cape Grace Hotel, which advertises itself as having "the Southern Hemisphere's biggest choice of whiskies" and the only whiskey sommelier on the continent. More than 500 brands are available at the bar, visited particularly by people from the many yachts anchored in the harbor just a few yards away. For the truly whiskey devout, there is the exclusive "Bascule Whisky Club," which offers a variety of perks, including your own lockable box, decorated with an engraved name plaque, in which to store your favorite whiskeys.

Even outside the tourist season between May and October, and during the early hours of the evening, the counter of the bar is often crowded with patrons who obviously don't need to pinch their pennies. They enjoy the sunsets here, often with the live music of a jazz band or a young bar singer in the background.

Upon reservation, the Bascule Bar offers diverse whiskey menus, and the expert kitchen of the hotel's Signal Restaurant creates sequences of dishes designed to pair well with the various spirits. There are also occasional whiskey tastings in small circles, usually focusing on rarer types.

A glass of the bar's most expensive single-malt whiskey, a 50-year-old Glenfiddich, will run you no less than 1,200 euros. Of course, there are also all of the usual kinds available for the usual bar prices. The whiskey sommelier, who trained in Scotland, gladly provides information about the rarer bottles and unusual producers. Not without pride, he'll also demonstrate the astonishing quality of South Africa's own award-winning whiskeys, such as Bain's.

Address Cape Grace Hotel, West Quay Road, V&A Waterfront, Cape Town 8002, Tel +27/214107100, www.capegrace.com | **Getting there** By public transit: Bus 104/106/107, Amsterdam stop; "Hop on-Hop off" bus, Aquarium stop | **Hours** Daily 10am–1am | **Tip** The V&A Waterfront Historical Walking Tour provides information about the era before the waterfront became a glittering shopping and amusement center. Tours start daily at 11am from the Chavonnes Battery Museum (Tel +27/214166230).

8 The Baxter
Cape Town's most versatile stage

"The Baxter," as the Capetonians call the theater in Rondebosch, the university district, is an important social and cultural center for the city. Five stages are available for plays, cabaret, classical and popular music, jazz, and dance. The biggest one seats 666 people. Theater, comedy, and dance festivals take place here every year. Students and theatrical trainees study, practice, and experiment in the studios and auxiliary rooms. There are workshops for amateurs and children, and the Ikhwezi Outreach program aims to bring culture to the socially disadvantaged in the townships. Jazz bands often strike up during the afternoon in the garden behind the multi-storied and architecturally sophisticated brick building.

The Baxter also offers a variety of gastronomic offerings: there's the Long Bar, which features tapas and wine; an unpretentious "grab and go" eatery; and a dignified restaurant called Act that serves dinner before the performances.

Despite its largely relaxed atmosphere, the Baxter can lay claim to being an important venue for political and avant-garde theater: ever since its opening in 1977, the house has identified itself as a "home for progressive South African theater." It was named after Cape Town's former mayor William D. Baxter (1868–1960), a native of Scotland who gave the university a rich endowment under the condition that it be used primarily to "develop and cultivate the arts in Cape Town and the adjacent districts."

Especially during apartheid, the Baxter was considered a significant alternative to the state-run Artscape Theatre Centre, where many pieces were regularly censored or banned by the government. Owned by the university, the Baxter was able to take advantage of its "academic freedom" to frequently present pieces critical of the regime.

Address Baxter Theatre Centre, 2 Main Road, Rondebosch, Cape Town 7701, Tel +27/216857880, www.baxter.co.za | **Getting there** By car: via N2 (Nelson Mandela Boulevard), turn right onto M3, exit 7, turn left to Woolsack Drive; at the end of the street, turn right onto Baxter Road, left onto Burg Road, and left onto Main Road. By public transit: Golden Arrow bus, Baxter Theatre stop; Metrorail, Red Line, Rondebosch Station. | **Hours** Box office 9am–1pm and 2–5pm | **Tip** Rondebosch Common Nature Reserve, in Rosebank, with its "Cape flats sand fynbos" (a biome peculiar to Cape Town) is under threat of being shut down, and is worth a visit.

9 Bay Harbour Market
A market that likes to celebrate

The biggest and most bustling fishing harbor on the peninsula can be found in Hout Bay, a charming coastal village with 20,000 inhabitants. The Dutchman Jan van Riebeeck, who had established a harbor in Table Bay in 1652, heard that the adjacent bay was rich in timber (*hout* means "wood" in Dutch), and had it developed by his crew.

Here, especially snook, but also lobsters are caught for the Cape Town market and the local restaurants. The center of the harbor is the big cooperative fish factory. Other fish factories have had to close down in recent years due to economic conditions, leaving a number of large warehouses vacant. One of them, at the very end of the harbor, was secured in 2012 by two businessmen, promoters, and friends, Anthony Stroebel and Paul Rutzen. Together they installed one of the most lively, creative, and beautiful markets in the entire Cape region. Even for many Cape Town residents, this market right on the waterfront is still an inside tip, although, since opening, it has already become something of a local institution.

More than 100 vendors can be found here, selling African handicrafts, unusual fashion articles, vintage treasures, and eco home decor, as well as outlandish food stands promoting culinary delicacies, wine tastings, and beer right out of the barrel. Live musicians play mostly exotic music in one corner of the gigantic rebuilt warehouse. Sometimes there are dance and theater performances as well, and concerts take place regularly.

Near the Bay Harbour Market, you can stroll through the harbor, with its multitude of alleyways and courtyards, where you'll find the eccentric little Fishermen's Chapel and the Fish on the Rocks snack bar, which looks a bit run-down but is said to have the best fish and chips in Cape Town.

Address 31 Harbour Road, Hout Bay, Cape Town 7806, Tel +27/825705997, www.bayharbour.co.za | **Getting there** By car: from Cape Town via the M6, exit onto Princess Street at the traffic circle, continue to the next traffic circle and take the first exit onto Harbour Road | **Hours** Fri 5–9pm, Sat and Sun 9:30am–4pm | **Tip** Mariner's Wharf restaurant, standing on gigantic wooden stilts on Hout Bay's broad beach, is known for its fresh lobster. In the morning, you can take a boat from the harbor to Duiker Island (the tour lasts for about an hour), home to several thousand so-called South-African sea lions, belonging to the marine mammal family Otariidae (eared seals and sea lions).

10 The Beach Cabins
Newfound symbols of freedom

You can find these brightly painted little cabins on the beaches at Muizenberg, Fish Hoek, and St. James. In St. James, they're right next to the large artificial tidal pool cemented into the rocky ocean, in which you can go swimming even when the surf is strong.

Today, the bathing cabins are rented by the season – a fact that is strongly criticized. Because whoever manages to get ahold of such a rental, where one can store all of one's bathing equipment and apparel, doesn't let go of it very easily. The waiting list for one of these gems is accordingly long.

Nonetheless, these picturesque Victorian cabanas are also a symbol of freedom. For open access to the beaches and thus also to these structures on wooden stilts wasn't always possible. At the end of the 19th century, the beach at Muizenberg in particular, which extends for miles along False Bay, was the summer stomping ground of affluent Capetonians, as Camps Bay is today. During the apartheid era, the beaches on the eastern section of the Cape peninsula were reserved exclusively for whites.

The water at False Bay will invite you to go swimming, as it is calmer than on the west coast of the Cape peninsula, and is a few degrees warmer all year long. On the flip side of the coin, due to the multitude of sea lions, there are often sharks in False Bay, which is 25 miles wide. However, there is also an ingenious early-warning system of shark flags in various colors, which indicate the level of danger.

The bay got its name from the frequent mistakes made by sailors trying to round Africa's southernmost point: they cast their anchors in False Bay, believing they had already arrived in Cape Bay.

Address Main Road, St. James, Cape Town 7945 | Getting there By car: take M3/M4. By public transit: Metrorail red line, Muizenberg or St. James station | Hours You can see the beach cabins year-round; with a little bit of luck, some of them might even be vacant and open | Tip A couple miles north of Muizenberg in the Rondevlei saltwater lagoon – an avian paradise declared a wildlife sanctuary in 1952 – there are hippopotami, which you can see from a boat.

11 The Bird Clinic
A bird in need is a friend indeed

Penguins are patient patients. And this is good, because it sometimes takes a while for them to be taken from the little cage that serves as a waiting room into the treatment room of this unusual animal protection center. Here at the headquarters of the South African Foundation for the Conservation of Coastal Birds (SANCCOB) in the Table View District, veterinarians and keepers tend to a multitude of broken wings and legs, feathers contaminated with oil, and other avian maladies.

The spacious grounds, which house numerous cages, dens, huts, a small artificial pond, and the foundation's main building, is a refuge for all kinds of local seabirds. The focus is on the South-African black-footed penguin, a species threatened by extinction.

Some 2,500 birds a year are treated at SANCCOB; both wildlife organizations and Good Samaritans bring the injured or orphaned animals to the rehabilitation center.

There are sometimes large-scale operations in which all available forces are mobilized and volunteers are called upon – as was the case after June 23, 2000, when a tanker accident near Robben Island spilled gigantic quantities of oil into the ocean, threatening the penguins in their breeding season, of all times. In the end, almost 20,000 black-footed penguins were finally cleaned of the oil film and released back into the wild.

The foundation not only trains specialists, but also seeks public support. It thus often gives guided tours through the institute, where you can watch the feeding and nursing of the penguins and other seabirds close up, and inform yourself about the issues of bird protection.

The center also offers practical training to young people – a program in high demand.

Address South African Foundation for the Conservation of Coastal Birds, 22 Pentz Drive, Table View, Cape Town 7441, Tel +27/215576155 | **Getting there** By car: take N 1 (Table Bay Boulevard), exit 4, R 27 Marine Drive, turns into West Coast Road, turn right onto M 14 Blaauwberg Road, first street on the right onto Pentz Drive. By public transit: Bus T 01, Table View stop | **Hours** Always open, but only upon reservation for visitors | **Tip** Several times each month, Western Province Motor Club organizes car races at Killarney Race Track in Table View (Tel +27/215571639).

12 — Bloubergstrand Beach
Sunset in front of Table Mountain

From no other place in Cape Town can Table Mountain be as prominently seen as from Bloubergstrand Beach, north of the suburb of Milnerton and directly east of Robben Island, some four-and-a-half miles away. The beach received its name from the nearly 1000-foot-high Blouberg ("blue mountain") a couple miles farther inland. It totals five-and-a-half miles in length and is divided into sections of varied terrains. Here, long, white sand beaches are interspersed with rock formations and dune landscapes similar to the Baltic Coast.

In general, the wind is pretty strong, but there are also many sheltered spots along Beach Road that are easily accessible by car, and where parking is no problem. These are ideal places to sunbathe, and you can by all means go swimming, although the water is often no warmer than 60 degrees Fahrenheit, due to the Benguela current. The lengthy sand beach invites long walks, and for wave and wind surfers, this place is a paradise. Kitesurfing on the west side of the bay is a spectacle particularly worth seeing: in the blustery wind, the surfers tear along the waves at breakneck speed. National and international kitesurfing competitions are often held on the beach.

Bloubergstrand is also a historic location: in 1806, more than 5,000 British marines landed here, beat the advancing Dutch troops to a pulp at the Battle of Blouberg, and thus did away with Dutch colonial rule on the Cape.

Among the many dining and drinking options along the beach, one of the most unusual is the Blue Peter Hotel, with 27 rooms, a bar, and a restaurant. The special attraction here is a sloping lawn in front of the white building, upon which people sit at tables and on blankets to behold the exceptional sunset, accompanied by African music, good drinks, and passable food.

Address Blue Peter Hotel, 7 Popham Road, on the corner of Rancke Road, Bloubergstrand, Cape Town 7441, Tel +27/215541956, www.bluepeter.co.za | **Getting there** By car: take R 27 north via Milnerton, and turn onto M 14 in Table View; in Bloubergstrand, turn left onto Big Bay Boulevard and then onto Popham Road. By public transit: Bus 214/217, De Mist and Kleinbaai stop | **Hours** Open year-round, especially charming in the evenings | **Tip** On the Rocks restaurant, at 45 Stadler Road, is known for superb seafood. Plan a visit to Woodbridge Island, home to the Milnerton lighthouse, accessible by a wooden bridge.

13 Bo-Kaap
Cape Town's vibrant district

It's a piece of historic luck that this neighborhood is still standing. The white politicians of apartheid always found the pretty run-down Moslem Bo-Kaap quarter, inhabited mainly by people of Asian heritage, to be an eyesore that they would have loved to demolish, like District Six. Numerous initiatives in the city, and especially the energetic resistance on the part of the inhabitants of Bo-Kaap themselves (the so-called Cape Malays) were able to prevent this.

Today, this neighborhood, with its colorful little houses, mosques, and minarets on steep, narrow streets, is among the city's jewels. Thanks to its Cape Dutch and Edwardian styles of architecture, the area, one of Cape Town's oldest, radiates a charming blend of the 18th and 19th centuries. Artistic circles in particular consider it "in" to move into one of Bo-Kaap's cheerful houses.

Asian merchants and craftspeople were the first to settle down here, around 1760. Asian exiles and convicts, captured and brought to the Cape by the Dutch East India Company and who were permitted to acquire their own homes, started moving here around 1780. Only a small portion were from Malaysia; most of them came from Indonesia, Sri Lanka, and India. As Malayan was the predominant language in the Asian colonies, however, the terms "Cape Malayan" and "Cape Malay" became customary.

Nearly all of the arrivals were Moslems. The Auwal Mosque built in 1798 (see p. 20), the first of its kind in Cape Town, bears testimony to this. Many families of the approximately 60,000 Cape Malayans in the Cape Town metropolitan area still live in Bo-Kaap. They helped to shape the Afrikaans culture and the language of South Africa.

Address Bo-Kaap, between Buitengracht and Signal Hill, Cape Town 8001 | **Getting there** By public transit: Bus 101, Church or Leeuwen Street stop; "Hop on-Hop off" bus, Jewel Africa stop | **Tip** The little Bo-Kaap Museum, located in one of Cape Town's oldest houses, at 71 Wale Street, offers information about the quarter and the history of its inhabitants (open Mon–Sat 10am–5pm, Tel +27/214243846). The Cape Town Minstrel Carnival, which always takes place in Cape Town on January 2, commemorates the abolition of slavery in 1834 through the British administration and the freeing of some 39,000 slaves in Cape Town province.

14_ The Book Lounge
Read and let read

At the end of 2007, in the Gardens District on the edge of Cape Town's inner city, an independent bookstore opened and quickly gained popularity, thanks to its impressive concept: it offered not only a wide choice of South-African literature, but also international titles. Moreover, the annual Open Book Festival, cofounded by shop owner Mervyn Sloman, was brought to life here. In just a short time, the Book Lounge thus turned into a literary rendezvous, as well as one of Cape Town's most successful bookstores. You'll get expert advice from the shop's knowledgeable staff.

Every Saturday morning, a fairy-tale hour takes place, which awakens children's interest in reading through being read to. In the basement, you can relax on one of the numerous cozy sofas over an espresso from a small cafeteria. Readings are given here regularly at which both renowned and new authors present their latest works.

South-African literature has as many facets as the country itself. Many writers were strongly affected by the apartheid era, and it plays a great role in their works. Such famous authors as Nadine Gordimer, who won the Nobel Prize for Literature in 1991 and died in 2014, are of key significance in the literary scene, as are the poet Lesego Rampolokeng and the writer J. M. Coetzee, who was born in Cape Town and descended from an African family – just like André Brink. Coetzee, Brink, and the popular writer Breyten Breytenbach, from the Western Cape Province, are among the best-known South Africans writing in Afrikaans.

There are a total of eleven official languages in South Africa in which publications are issued; English and Afrikaans are the leading ones.

Address 71 Roeland Street, at Buitenkant Street, Gardens, Cape Town 8001, Tel +27/214622425, www.booklounge.co.za | **Getting there** By public transit: Bus 103, Roeland Street stop | **Hours** Mon–Fri 8:30am–7:30pm, Sat 9am–5pm, Sun 10am–4pm | **Tip** Exclusive Books on Victoria Wharf at the waterfront and Clarke's Bookshop on Long Street are recommended.

15 __ The Campus
A university rich in treasures

On his visit to South Africa in 2013, U.S. president Barack Obama gave a speech at the University of Cape Town (UCT). The historic rooms in South Africa's oldest university were the perfect stage for his address on the principle of Africa's future. On this occasion, Obama also lauded the beauty of UCT, with its picturesque location high above the city. The institution has a first-class reputation: for a long time, it has been the only African university included in the *Times Higher Education*, which ranks it as one of the 120 best universities in the world. Four Nobel Prize winners studied here: the physicians Max Theiler (prize in 1951) and Allan McLeod Cormack (1979), the chemist Aaron Klug (1982), and the writer J. M. Coetzee (2003).

The institution was founded in 1829 as South African College in the foothills of Table Mountain. It became a state university in 1918. The grand wide staircase to Jammie Plaza and Jameson Hall, with their imposing columned entrance, stand in the center of the large campus. A great part of student life takes place on the steps and the beautiful plazas between the institutes and the dormitories: it is here that the students study, discuss, celebrate, and demonstrate.

UCT has been considered a political university for a long time – meaning that it was in permanent confrontation with the government for ages. As early as almost 100 years ago, blacks were also allowed to study at UCT. While they remained an exception, the university became a stronghold in the struggle against apartheid during the 1980s, leading to police raids on the campus and violent confrontations between demonstrating students and security personnel. Currently, some 25,000 students are enrolled at UCT; almost one-fifth of them are from abroad, and only about one-third of them are white.

Address University of Cape Town, Rhodes Drive, Rondebosch, Cape Town 7700, www.uct.ac.za | **Getting there** By car: take N2 (Nelson Mandela Boulevard), turn right on M3 (Rhodes Drive), exit 7, turn right on Woolsack Drive, which turns into the North Entrance Road to the university. By public transit: Golden Arrow Bus, Rondebosch stop, then transfer to the UCT shuttle bus to the Upper Campus; Metrorail Red Line, Rosebank station, then take the UCT shuttle bus | **Hours** Guests will need to register in the visitors' office (Upper Campus); guided tours Mon–Fri, registration: Tel +27/216504556 or admissions@uct.ac.za | **Tip** The Kirstenbosch Craft Market, held on the last Sunday of every month (Kirstenbosch Stone Cottages, corner of Kirstenbosch Drive and Rhodes Avenue), has 190 craftspeople.

16 Canal Walk
South Africa's biggest shopping center

Century City, near the northern suburb of Milnerton, is a city within the city, hammered out of thin air in just a few years. Billions were invested in the project constructed in 1995 on a nearly 620-acre site amid canals and swamps. Besides 3,000 apartment houses in highly varied styles designed for 60,000 people, there are futuristic office towers with around 400,000 square meters of space. Numerous large companies have settled here. Vodacom resides in a gigantic neoclassical-style office building with a columned entrance.

The commercial core of Century City is Canal Walk, Africa's biggest shopping center, which opened in 2000. With its two partially glassed towers visible from afar, it is reminiscent of an oriental palace.

Many visitors say that Canal Walk tops all the malls they've ever seen, including those in the United States. The shopping center is crisscrossed by canals and the interior is filled with palm trees. Replicas of paintings by Michelangelo and Gauguin decorate some of the walls and ceilings.

Customers go shopping in gigantic arcades lined with more than 400 stores run by all of the internationally renowned retailers; there are also movie theaters, discotheques, bars and cafés, and, above all, a titanic food court with innumerable restaurants and snack counters. A project costing billions, Canal Walk is a world of consumption not far from the townships. The retail mecca has been particularly popular among Cape Town's middle class, with families spending entire days here.

Century City also includes Ratanga, a 50-acre amusement park that opened in 1998 and features water slides, a theater, a circus, and the "Cobra," a high-speed roller coaster that plunges down from a height of 115 feet.

Address Century City, Milnerton, Cape Town 7441, Tel +27/215553250, www.canalwalk.co.za | **Getting there** By car: take N1 in the direction of Paarl, about 6 miles northeast of the inner city, Sable Road exit, then continue down Century Boulevard to the large marked parking levels. Public transit: Bus T 01, Century City stop | **Hours** Daily 9am–9pm (the restaurants and bars close later), visitors' center Tel +27/215299699 | **Tip** Other big malls are Tyger Valley, in Bellville; Cavendish Center, in the southern suburb Claremont; Gardens Center, in the Gardens District; and of course the Waterfront.

17 — The Cape
A visit to the Cape of Good Hope

Despite the abundance of parking spots and good organization, the hustle and bustle at the Cape of Good Hope is considerable. But once you arrive at the always blustery end of the peninsula, you'll behold a fantastic panorama of the coastline. Until the Suez Canal was built in 1869, the ocean route to India went right past this point. For centuries seafarers thought of the Cape of Good Hope with yearning and fear. For it is here that the cold Benguela current and the warm Agulhas current converge, and that many ambitious dreams of expeditions and trade met their end in the tumultuous waters.

The composer Richard Wagner immortalized the seafarers' fears in his opera *The Flying Dutchman*. The work deals with the legendary figure of the Dutch captain Bernard Fokke, who, battling the primal forces of the tempest and the ocean at the Cape, curses God and nature. For this reason, he is damned to wander with his ghost ship across the seas for all eternity. The legend and the opera are products of fantasy, but the numerous shipwrecks at the stormy Cape were realities. Hundreds of sunken ships are lying at the bottom of the ocean beyond the rocks and beaches. Even after the lighthouse was built here, in 1859, the Cape still disappeared into the blackness of night during heavy fog and rain for about 900 hours a year.

If you climb to the top of the no-longer-operational lighthouse, you'll have a breathtaking view over the jagged coastline, solitary beaches, and the national park. At least part of the ascent can be accomplished by means of a small private mountain railway. On the six hiking tours in Cape National Park, you'll frequently run into ostriches, springboks, baboons, and countless birds, 200 species of which live here. However, keep a close eye out for snakes.

Address Entrance building to the National Park, M 65 Plateau Road, Simon's Town, Cape Town 7975; Buffelsfontein Visitor Centre (in the park): Tel +27/217809204, www.tmnp.co.za | **Getting there** By car: take M 3 in the direction of Muizenberg, then M 4 in the direction of Simon's Town and continue south; signs will lead you to the Cape of Good Hope | **Tip** Swimming and picnicking as well as fishing are permitted in the small bays and sandy beaches of Cape National Park. Particularly lovely and less populated are the pools at Buffels Bay (tour buses are not permitted to stop there).

18 _ The Cape Houses
Historic architecture on the Cape

Entering the thatched Schreuderhuis, built in 1709 with its little rooms and clay floors, is a tiny trip in a time machine. A friendly elderly lady wearing a typical 18th-century hood – and a number of layered dresses – will enjoy telling you about everyday life in colonial times. The first immigrants from the Netherlands, Germany, and France lived in the Spartan rooms without glass windows – with a fireplace in the kitchen, onion buds hanging from the ceiling, and simple furniture. All of them identified themselves as pioneers bringing civilization into the south of Africa by means of their culture and religion.

The Schreuderhuis is the oldest of four buildings maintained here in their original condition. Each one of them represents in its architecture and its interior decoration a different period of urban development. The houses, with their small front yards typical of their respective times, are the center of the Stellenbosch Village Museum, which opened in 1962.

The Blettermanhuis, constructed in 1789 by a magistrate named Hendrik Lodewyk Bletterman and far more comfortable than the one built by Schreuder, was a courthouse for a long time, then a school, and later a police station.

How quickly the Boers attained affluence can be seen at Grosvenor House, which is almost pompously equipped with fine English furniture. The two-story manor was built in 1803.

The Kruithaus, from 1771, is said to be the only warehouse still preserved from that time. The Dutch East India Company dominated economic life here: the building was used as an armory and for military training.

In addition to the period houses, a collection of toys and dolls from the last two centuries, including a toy train set, also belongs to the Stellenbosch Museum.

Address Stellenbosch Village Museum, 18 van Ryneveld Street, Stellenbosch 7600, Tel +27/218872902, www.stelmus.co.za | **Getting there** By car: take N2 out of the city, R310 to Stellenbosch, follow signs in the direction of Dorp Street, turn left on Drostdy Road | **Hours** Sep–Mar, Mon–Sat 9am–5pm, Sun 10am–4pm; April–Aug, Mon–Sat 9am–5pm, Sun 10am–1pm | **Tip** The colorful Oom Samie Se Winkel general store on Dorp Street offers a dizzying array of porcelain, delicacies, souvenirs, wines, tools, and textiles.

19 Cape to Cuba
In homage to Che Guevara

Kitschy would be an understatement in describing Cape to Cuba; nevertheless, the restaurant has a special appeal. Situated next to the tracks of Kalk Bay Station with a panorama of the picturesque harbor, one encounters a hodgepodge of treasured odds and ends and devotional objects having to do with Cuba and its revolutionary hero Che Guevara.

Entering through a kind of wooden shed, you'll find yourself in a front yard with tables on white sand. Continue walking into the tall wooden huts with corrugated roofs, and you won't believe your eyes: it's as if you've been transported to Cuba, whichever way you turn. Though not always precisely authentic, the rooms are chock full of colorful decorations. Amongst the tables, palms, and flowers you'll encounter the image of Che Guevara on paintings, photos, and in plaster, next to countless revolutionary posters, figures of saints, parts of old Cuban cars, a gigantic humidor, references to Ernest Hemingway, straw hats, Caribbean outfits, expansive chandeliers, cages with stuffed parrots, and whole batteries of rum bottles. Uninterrupted Cuban Salsa rhythms play in the background, and there is live music on weekends.

Señora Deona cooks mainly Cuban cuisine with lots of fresh fish and a strong Cajun influence. After a lengthy trip to Cuba, when she and her husband fell in love with the Caribbean island, the two of them opened their restaurant in 1999 in Kalk Bay, where they also live. The drinks are based predominantly on Cuban rum. Favorites include the mojitos, lauded as the best on the Cape, and the daiquiris.

Incidentally, almost all of Cape to Cuba's furnishings and decorations are for sale. And smoking Cuban cigars is explicitly permitted.

Address 165 Main Road, Cape Town, 7990, Tel +27/217881566, www.capetocuba.com | **Getting there** By car: take M3/M4 via Muizenberg to Kalk Bay. By public transit: Metrorail Red Line, Kalk Bay Station | **Hours** Tue–Sat 11:30am–4:30pm and 6–10:30pm, bar open until 11:30pm | **Tip** On the other side of Main Road, you'll run into the Olympia Café, famed for its homemade cakes. The Brass Bell in Kalk Bay railroad station offers no less than five restaurants and three pubs, and an opportunity to sit outside at the harbor or take a dip between courses in a tidal pool. Harbour House, situated directly above the harbor, is a first-class restaurant. Kalk Bay is famous for its numerous offbeat antique shops and galleries.

20 __ The Castle
A sense of colonial times in the Castle of Good Hope

Built between 1666 and 1679 by soldiers, sailors, and slaves at the command of the Dutch East India Company, the Castle of Good Hope is the oldest intact colonial building in South Africa. It took the place of a wooden fort built previously by Commander Jan van Riebeeck on the Grand Parade Quarter. One peculiarity of the castle is that it was never attacked throughout its centuries-long history, and despite all historic turbulence, it is still the headquarters of the Western Cape Military Commando – meaning that it is used by the military even today. The changing of the guard and the key delivery in the morning by soldiers in historic uniforms are worth seeing.

The Dutch constructed the castle as a five-pointed star – a pentagonal fortress with a bastion at each corner. They utilized granite from the base of Table Mountain, shells used in making mortar from Robben Island (transported with great effort by slaves on ships), and wood from Hout Bay. The 590-foot-long and nearly 33-foot-high fortress wall and the moat surrounding the castle were then added.

Inside, various administration and residential buildings were erected, as the fortress was not only used for military purposes: the crews of ships on their way to India rested here. On the order of Governor Simon van der Stel, the entry originally facing the sea quite close to the water was moved sideways due to frequent flooding of the courtyard. It is still there today. The resulting portal, completed here in 1684 at the main entrance below the bell tower, shows a lion with seven arrows symbolizing the provinces of the Netherlands outside Europe at that time. Due to the expansion of the Cape Town harbor and constant new earth fills in the 1940s, the location of the castle has shifted farther into the city.

Address Darling and Castle Streets, City, Cape Town 8000, Tel +27/217871084, www.castleofgoodhope.co.za | **Getting there** Public transit: Bus 102, Castle stop; "Hop on-Hop off" bus, Castle of Good Hope stop | **Hours** Daily 9am–4pm, last entry 3:30pm; guided tours available Mon–Sat 11am, 12pm, and 2pm, book tours at Tel +27/217871249 | **Tip** The castle includes the Cape Town Military Museum, which houses the permanent exhibition of the William Fehr Collection, with African motifs by European artists, as well as African furniture – and the Good Hope Gallery for contemporary African art.

21 Chapman's Peak Drive
A toll well spent

You'll pay a fee to get on Chapman's Peak Drive – but it might be the best money you spend on your entire trip to South Africa. It's simply one of the most spectacular and entrancing coastal highways in the entire world and you'll never forget this five-and-a-half-mile stretch of road along the Atlantic coast between Hout Bay and Noordhoek. If you pull over to linger in one of the little parking spots along the way (and you must), you won't be able to get enough of what you behold.

Between 1915 and 1922, seven hundred men, most of them convicts, chopped and dynamited Chapman's Peak Drive into the cliffs, at those places in the rock formations where soft sandstone lies on top of hard granite. It was a bold undertaking that was always on the verge of being given up on, but was finally completed and named after the English seafarer John Chapman, who, in 1607, had been the first to explore Hout Bay.

In 2000, the coastal highway had to be entirely closed off and renovated due to continually falling rocks and numerous fatal accidents. It was expanded and equipped with steel safety nets; some of the rocks were cemented in; and a kind of avalanche tunnel was constructed. At the end of 2003, it was reopened as a toll road, with collection booths positioned only on the Hout Bay side. There are still falling rocks, however, and driving on this highway is always at your own risk.

Two of the biggest annual sporting events on the Cape are carried out on Chapman's Peak Drive: the 68-mile-long Cape Argus Cycle Race, which draws some 35,000 competitors, and the so-called Two Oceans Marathon, which, with its 35 miles, is always a prominent sports spectacle. Runners who aren't quite up to such a long distance can opt for the half-marathon of about 13 miles.

Address Coastal highway between Hout Bay and Noordhoek, Cape Town 7806, Tel +27/217918220 (toll station), www.chapmanspeakdrive.co.za | **Getting there** By car: take M6 from Cape Town | **Tip** At the end of Chapman's Peak Drive, the imposing miles-long Noordhoek Beach becomes visible.

22 The Clock Tower
Former residence of the Port Captain

Originally white, then red for decades, and now yellow, the historic Clock Tower, built in 1882 in Cape Town's old harbor, changes with the spirit of the times. Its current sunny shade is a sign of the city's artistic freedom as the "World Design Capital." The old tower, whose original clock came from Edinburgh and still keeps time, stands at the border between the Victoria and the Alfred Basin. As the economy prospered, the harbor became too small and Duncan Dock was built farther to the east, followed by the even larger Ben Schoenman Dock. As a result, the two original basins grew decreasingly important.

Up until this time, however, the Clock Tower was the heart of Cape Town's harbor. The three-story octagonal tower started out as the seat of the Port Captain. Every ship had to pass this "authority." The precise clock with its mighty clockwork on the top of the Victorian-style tower was the standard for all arriving and departing ships. Furthermore, the tower contained equipment to measure the exact level of the tide. The length of a ship's stopover could thus be controlled and billed. Signal flags, Morse devices, and telescopes were also stored in the tower. The second floor was equipped with a 360-degree mirror, so that nothing escaped the Port Captain's attention.

After construction of the bright blue Port Captain's building with its two conspicuous gables was completed in 1904, the function of the Clock Tower became purely technical. The Port Captain's significance at that time is evidenced by the very first telephone connection in Cape Province – with a direct wire from the harbor to the central post office on Darling Street.

In 1997, the run-down Clock Tower was fully restored to its original condition.

Address V&A Waterfront, Cape Town 8001, Tel +27/214252426 | Getting there Public transit: Bus 104, Nobel Square stop; "Hop on-Hop off" bus, Clock Tower stop | Hours Daily 9am–9pm | Tip Right next to the Clock Tower is the Nelson Mandela Gateway where a multimedia presentation plays before the ferry leaves for Robben Island. A visit is worthwhile even without the voyage to the former prison that once housed Nelson Mandela.

23 — The Colonial Houses
Strolling along the Historic Mile

Simonstad, built by the Dutch in 1687 because of its sheltered location as a harbor for the ships of the Dutch East India Company and named after the governor of that era, Simon van der Stel, was conquered in 1795 by the British, who expanded it into a naval base starting in 1814 and called it Simon's Town. Simon's Town remained an important British naval base up to the mid-1950s. Today, the harbor is a central base of the South-African navy, with an adjoining wharf for repairing warships.

The so-called Historic Mile in the center of Simon's Town, St. George's Street, bears witness to the city's boom time, when the British enlarged it in Victorian style. The more than 20 colorful partly wooden houses, with their playful facades and broad balconies facing the main street, are a fascinating testimony to this epoch.

Admiralty House and Palace Barracks are particularly noteworthy, as is the old residence of the governor dating from 1777, now occupied by the Simon's Town Museum, which documents the city's architecture and history, including details of the apartheid era. The museum was founded in 1977 by the local historical society.

Simon's Town has a small waterfront with fish restaurants and numerous shops and galleries, especially around Jubilee Square, close to the harbor. Here also stands the bronze monument to the Great Dane named Just Nuisance, who was the canine mascot and a "member" of the British Navy during World War II and thus came to fame and honor.

Simon's Town is the southern terminus of the Metrorail, which sometimes during the summer months uses trains that are a bit more comfortable than the typical ones, and even have restaurants.

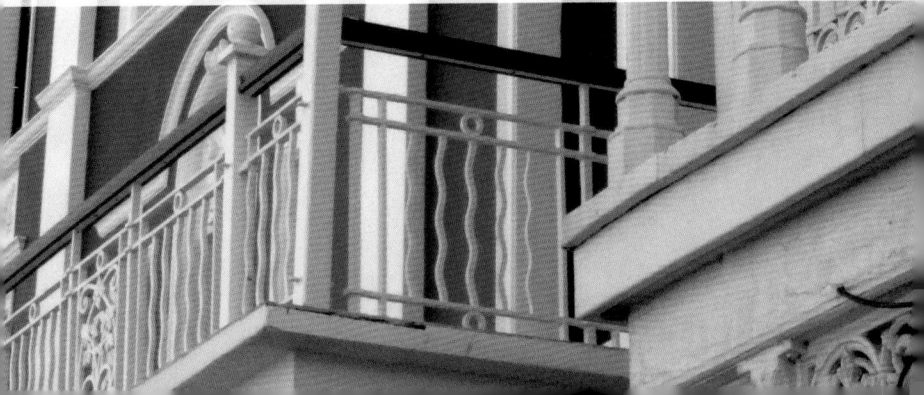

Address St. George's Street, Simon's Town, Cape Town 7975, www.simonstown.com | Getting there By car: take M 4. By public transit: Metrorail Red Line, Simon's Town station (last stop) | Tip Boyes Drive is an alternative route between Muizenberg and Simon's Town, way up on the mountain and accessible from M 4. The toy museum on St. George's Street and the Naval Museum depicting the history of the navy base are both quite interesting. On Seal Island in False Bay, you can watch whales from June to November.

24 The Colonial Monument
Where Vasco da Gama is commemorated

Although the Portuguese explorer Bartolomeu Diaz was the first European to sail around the southernmost point of Africa, in 1488, it was Vasco da Gama whom Portugal's king Manuel I commissioned for the thorough exploration of this important trade route to India. Da Gama went down in history with this accomplishment, whereas Diaz remained obscure. On the Cape, however, both of these seafaring pioneers are commemorated, even if in different places. The Diaz monument – in the classical form of a stone cross – is near the visitors' center of Cape National Park. The very similar da Gama monument was erected near the beach in Buffels Bay below the lighthouse. Both monuments were donated in 1965 by the Portuguese government. Below the Vasco da Gama monument are a number of small solitary beaches.

It was da Gama who, on a secret mission in 1497, definitively opened the important seaway to India for his country, thereby enhancing Portugal's status as a world power. For nearly one hundred years, it was mainly the Portuguese who tried to eliminate Arabian, Persian, Turkish, and Venetian middlemen from the trade of Asia's precious spices by means of a new seaway. Finally, on May 20, 1498, da Gama landed on the Malabar Coast in India. That was the first time a European ship reached India by sea. With further Portuguese seafaring missions, Africa also played a secondary role. Vasco da Gama's ships lay at anchor one single time for a period of 16 days in St. Helena Bay. In his log, he wrote about "men with brown skin" who ate sea lions, gazelles, and roots, as well as about the fascinating fauna, to which, astonishingly, even penguins belonged. His records are the first descriptions of life on the Cape, where the first Dutch colonists were to land more than 150 years later.

Address Entrance building to the National Park, M 65 Plateau Road, Simon's Town, Cape Town 7975; Buffelsfontein Visitor Centre (in the park): +27/217809204, www.tmnp.co.za | **Getting there** By car: take M3 in the direction of Muizenberg, then M 4 in the direction of Simon's Town, and farther south. Signs lead to the "Da Gama Cross" | **Hours** Oct–Mar, daily 6am–6pm, Apr–Sep, 7am–5pm (Caution: if you stay longer than permitted in Cape National Park, you will be fined) | **Tip** You should take a look at the cave "Antonie's Gate" at the edge of Buffels Bay (near the visitors' center in Cape National Park). According to legend, the escaped slave Lalu Abdl Dea Koasa, to whom spiritual powers are attributed, lived here in the 18th century.

25 The Crypt
Jazz beneath Desmond Tutu's church

This is presumably the only crypt in the world where jazz is played in the midst of the memorial plaques of the departed. Such a thing could only occur in a liberal environment like St. George's Cathedral, which was once presided over by the former archbishop of Cape Town, Desmond Tutu. The Crypt Jazz Restaurant, in which excellent cuisine is combined with good music, is located on the side of the church, in a basement vault supported on columns with great semicircular arches. Artistically formed marble plaques are set into the walls everywhere: behind the tables, the wardrobe, the stage with the instruments, and the bar. They harbor graves from the second half of the 19th century, in which venerable citizens of the town, officers, seafarers, politicians, and clerics rest. International and Cape Town jazz is played in the Crypt, with a different act performing every night.

The imposing house of worship itself, which is traditionally financed exclusively by its congregation, donations, and various ventures such as the quaint secondhand bookstore right next door, is the principle seat of the Anglican Church of South Africa. It was built in 1834, elevated to the status of a cathedral as early as 1848, and comprehensively renovated in 1901 by the British-South African architect Herbert Baker in the neo-Gothic style.

The cathedral was always a hotbed of resistance against the apartheid regime personified by Desmond Tutu. For preaching against racial segregation and state terror, Tutu was awarded the Nobel Peace Prize in 1984. He still sermonizes regularly at St. George, but if you would like to hear him speak, you'll have to get up early, as he prefers to hold services during the morning hours.

Address The Crypt Jazz Restaurant, 1 Wale Street, City, Cape Town 8001, Tel +27/796834658, www.thecryptjazz.com | **Getting there** Public transit: Bus 106/107, Groote Kerk stop; "Hop on-Hop off" bus, St. George's Cathedral stop | **Hours** Live jazz: Tue–Thu 7–10pm, Fri and Sat 8–11pm, tickets through Tel 079/6834658; restaurant: Tue–Sat 5pm–midnight | **Tip** Don't miss the big leaded-glass window at the northern portal of the church. The frequent concerts are highly recommended as well; the church's acoustics are excellent.

26 De Waal Park
Green oasis below Molteno Reservoir

Since the Friends of De Waal Park took the initiative in 2008 to reactivate this lovely area with its rich tradition in the center of the city, the park has experienced a renaissance, and a growing number of Capetonians are rediscovering the green oasis. Here, you can relax under dense treetops in the warmer months, make a date for a picnic in the area around the Victorian fountain, or attend one of the numerous summer concerts of classical music, rock, or jazz.

In 1877, John Molteno, who was prime minister at the time, commissioned the Molteno Dam as part of a huge infrastructure project on the lower slope of Table Mountain. It included the creation of a reservoir with a basin nearly 1000 feet long and 330 feet wide, then the largest in the city, and still serving parts of the City Bowl. In 1881, the first electric power plant in all of South Africa – was put into operation at Cape Town.

The park, which was situated in the vacant area between the Molteno Reservoir and two other smaller reservoirs below Camp Street, opened in 1895 at the behest of former mayor David Christiaan de Waal (1889–1890), who was a close friend of Cecil Rhodes. It was de Waal's idea to provide Cape Town with hundreds of new trees. As early as 1877, the city had bought the Oranjezicht farm, which occupied the entire territory below Table Mountain, from the van Breda family, and divided it into three parts. A short time after the park's opening, a wall with wrought-iron arches and artistically decorated entries was installed. The Victorian fountain in the middle of the park followed, in 1898. In 1905, the Scotch music pavilion (originally made for the big Cape Town exhibition at Green Point) was added, in which a military band played every Sunday afternoon for many years.

Address Upper Orange Road, Oranjezicht, Cape Town 8001, Tel +27/214002521 | **Getting there** By car: via Buitengracht and New Church Street onto Kloof Nek Road, then turn left into Camp Street up to the park. By public transit: Bus 103, Lower Reservoir and De Waal Park stops | **Hours** Sept – Mar, daily 6:30am – 8pm, April – Aug, daily 7am – 6pm | **Tip** The city's biggest and loveliest park is the Company's Garden. Green Point Urban Park at the stadium and Trafalgar Park in Woodstock also are very pleasant.

27 De Waterkant
Free to be you and me

If there is one metropolis in Africa where international jet setters, Hollywood stars, fashion icons, and filmmakers sometimes converge, it's doubtlessly Cape Town, with its lively arts and music scene and dynamic nightlife. In 2014, the *New York Times* called the "Mother City" one of the ten hippest cities around the globe. That same year, Cape Town was named World Design Capital.

The quarter in which this creative vibe is most apparent is De Waterkant. In this picturesque part of Green Point near the Moslem quarter, Bo-Kaap, you will find many interesting galleries, antiques stores, designer shops, bars, clubs, and restaurants. Particularly in the evenings, things get very lively in the surroundings of the Cape Quarter shopping center. Nowhere in Cape Town does one sense the broad scope of the South-African "rainbow nation" as intensely as in this spirited neighborhood.

The term *rainbow nation* is attributed to former archbishop Desmond Tutu. The rainbow, however, is also the worldwide symbol of gay pride and stands for tolerance and freedom. Despite liberal laws, gays and lesbians have a tough time in South Africa's still largely traditional society, so De Waterkant is famous far and wide as an oasis for alternative lifestyles.

The metropolis of Cape Town definitely has a very animated LGBTQ (lesbian, gay, bisexual, transgender, queer/questioning) scene, with its own periodicals and facilities. The city is proud to publish a "Pink Guide" to help visitors find what they're looking for.

Cape Town advertises itself as the site of the annual Mother City Queer Project, the biggest gay festival of its kind in all of Africa. The stronghold of the celebrators is De Waterkant, also nicknamed "Gaybourhood" or "Pink Village" by the natives.

Address Cape Quarter, 27 Somerset Road, De Waterkant, Cape Town 8005, Tel +27/214211111, www.capequarter.co.za | **Getting there** By public transit: Bus 108/109, Alfred Road stop | **Hours** Stores: Mon–Fri 9am–6pm, Sat 9am–4pm, Sun 10am–2pm, restaurants and bars differ | **Tip** Bubbles Bar with its "Disco Divas" cabaret, at 125a Waterkant Street, is not only a meeting place for the transvestite community – all are welcome (Tel +27/218010501).

28 The Design Centre
Watch artists at work in Montebello

Cape Town is a city brimming with creativity: in 2014, it was named the official world capital of design. Ateliers and studios are strewn all over the metropolis. At the Montebello Design Centre artists' colony you can talk with and watch some 20 artisans at work. Far away from the big city's tumult, the artistic center, in the shadow of old and mighty camphor trees, supplies a contemplative atmosphere and is seldom crowded. The center was founded by the Michaelis, an entrepreneurial German immigrant family. The family gave the premises – which belong to the University of Cape Town – an endowment on condition that it be used to promote the work of young designers and artists.

In the simple little cottages and the large main building, designers of jewelry and textiles, painters, photographers, sculptors, and filmmakers establish their workshops, generally for one year. A branch of the David Krut Project – an initiative and platform for contemporary South African art – also has a space in Montebello, in addition to branches in New York and Johannesburg. The gallery offers mainly excellent prints. You can purchase a large spectrum of smaller and larger works either directly from the artists or in the central gallery.

There is also a kind of souvenir store, which offers unusual mementos and handiwork of noticeably high quality. The café restaurant, Gardener's Cottage, located in the main building, once harbored a brewery and then a porcelain factory, and is a beloved local breakfast and lunch spot.

Every Friday morning, the grounds are turned into a lively marketplace. The Mielie Food Garden and Organic Market sells regional agrarian products. Proceeds are passed on to community gardens and small farms in the townships.

Address Montebello Design Centre, 31 Newlands Avenue, Newlands, Cape Town 7708, Tel +27/216850676, www.montebello.co.za | **Getting there** By car: take M3, Newlands exit | **Hours** Tue–Fri 10am–5pm, Sat 10am–2pm | **Tip** Josephine Mill, on Boundary Road in Newlands, is Cape Town's oldest surviving water mill, dating from 1840 – it features shops, a bar, a restaurant, and a mill museum (Tel. +27/216864939, www.josephinemill.co.za).

29 — The Diamond House
A precious history presented in a precious home

South Africa's association with diamonds goes back 150 years. In 1866, when a little Boer boy exploring the banks of the Orange River found a particularly glittery stone that turned out to be a 20-carat diamond, jewel fever broke out across the southern part of the continent, including the Cape. A run on diamonds began, as did a struggle for claims and digging rights. A powerful industry arose, linked with the names Cecil Rhodes, De Beers, and Oppenheimer, and along with it came merciless syndicates, ruthless exploitation, and monstrous wealth. The worldwide diamond trade became one of South Africa's main industries and sources of income.

Since 1993, the jewelry store Prins & Prins Diamonds, one of the top names in Cape Town's diamond trade, has resided in the 18th-century bourgeois Hugenot House (built in 1752 and restored in the 1980s), which for decades had served as the office for the wines of the Franschhoek region. At the beginning of 2014, on the lower level of the old urban villa, Prins & Prins opened the private Museum of Gems and Jewellery, which offers insights into the history of diamonds on the Cape.

The owner of the firm, Petr Prins, or one of his employees often guides visitors through the little museum concealed behind the workshop downstairs. With a doctorate in geology and chemistry and experience as a jeweler going back to 1982, Prins leads his visitors entertainingly and impressively through the turbulent evolution of the South-African diamond trade. In connection with the house's own diamond workshop and goldsmith, he adds an introduction to gemology. You can watch some of the 20 or so employees grinding diamonds in the rough, and see designers creating pieces of jewelry on the upper floors of the Hugenot House.

Address Museum of Gems and Jewellery, Huguenot House, 66 Loop on the corner of Hout Street, City, Cape Town 8001, Tel +27/214221090, www.prinsandprins.com | **Getting there** By public transit: Bus 101, Mid Long Street stop, or Bus 105, Strand Street stop; "Hop on-Hop off" bus, Long Street Tour Office stop | **Hours** Mon–Fri 9am–5pm, Sat 9am–1pm (no reservation necessary) | **Tip** The elegant Cape Town Diamond Museum, behind the clock tower at the waterfront, is a must-see for those looking to familiarize themselves with the history of the "world's most precious gem."

30 The Disa Park Towers
Where perspectives collide

There are hardly any buildings that arouse as much emotional unrest among the Capetonians as the three Disa Park towers, in the district of Vredehoek. The reason is easily grasped: the trio of round, 17-story high-rises hits you in the eye when you admire Table Mountain with the city stretched out picturesquely at its base. The Blinkwater, Platteklip, and Silverstroom towers, each of them 180 feet high, are immortalized on countless panoramic postcards of the 3500-foot-high mountain, with its world-famous plateau.

When many locals speak of the towers, they refer to them as an "urban planning crime" and a "disgrace" to their city, making fun of the structures as the "Pepper Pots" or "Tampon Towers." The South-African architecture critic Barry Washkansky called them "ugly, oversized phalli." It's no wonder that there already have been a number of attempts to demolish the abominable residential complexes. A poll taken by the local newspaper *Cape Times* in 2010 showed a clear majority among its readers in favor of demolition. As early as 10 years prior, there had been a citizens' initiative to tear down at least the upper floors. The owners and tower tenants were able to avert this on legal grounds.

Those who actually live in the towers' apartments are downright crazy about the cylindrical buildings, which were erected in the 1960s, during apartheid, by the construction firm Murray and Roberts. Apart from their phenomenal view of Cape Town's skyline, the bay, and the harbor, the towers also offer many luxury amenities, including a swimming pool, tennis and squash courts, and a grill area. For young middle-class families who can rent an apartment in one of the buildings for the equivalent of 750 euros, the presence of a kindergarten and a nursery school is particularly attractive.

Address Disa Park, 36 Chelmsford Road, Vredehoek, Cape Town 8001, www.disapark.co.za | **Getting there** By car: take Buitenkant Street toward the castle. By public transit: Bus 101, Exner Avenue stop | **Hours** Visits start at 10am on workdays upon reservation with the administration; some apartments are also rented to tourists | **Tip** In 2012, Cape Town's oldest farm was reactivated and expanded into an ecological agricultural operation with a store and a market called Oranjezicht City Farm. It is adjacent to Homestead Park, at the corner of Upper Orange Street and Sidmouth Avenue.

31 The District Six Museum
A sinister chapter of apartheid

The sixth district of Cape Town, which was established in 1867 and inhabited mainly by freed slaves, workers, merchants, European immigrants, and artists, developed in just a few years into a vivacious and liberal center of the city. Yet this thriving, multiethnic district near the inner city was deemed a run-down, diseased, and criminal area by the conservative Boers, and by the turn of the century, black South Africans living there were being deported to the townships.

In the 1960s, the entire district was supposed to disappear completely from the map of the city. The so-called Group Areas Act of 1950 served as the legal basis for forcibly driving out and resettling people of various skin colors who had lived in District Six for generations, and arbitrarily declared the entire district a "white residential territory." Some 60,000 people were relocated into the Cape Flats and gigantic barracks settlements way outside the city gates.

In 1966, the first bulldozers came and leveled District Six to the ground. Those in power left only the churches and mosques standing, out of fear of riots. In the 1980s, the whites located the gigantic Cape Technikon, belonging to the University of Cape Town, right where the center of an organically developed district once had been.

The District Six Museum in a former church not far from the destroyed area impressively documents the crimes of apartheid and will give you an authentic impression of past life in this quarter.

Although the area was to have been settled on by whites, large parts of it remain vacant to this day. A few years ago, new houses started being built, making it possible for former inhabitants and their children to come back.

Address The District Six Museum, 25a Buitenkant Street, Zonnebloem, Cape Town 7925, Tel +27/214667200, www.districtsix.co.za | **Getting there** By public transit: Bus 103, Lower Buitenkant stop; "Hop on-Hop off" bus, District Six Museum stop | **Hours** Mon–Sat 9am–4pm (tours guided by former inhabitants of the quarter) | **Tip** Plan to spend some time exploring the District Six area. Even today, it imparts an oppressive atmosphere – especially when you've visited the museum beforehand.

32 Evita se Perron
A theater for Pieter-Dirk Uys

South-African whites can be proud of many of their writers and artists who resisted the racist apartheid regime. Most of them are hardly in the spotlight anymore, but Pieter-Dirk Uys, one of the most iridescent South-African artists, still is. Many pictures and letters attest to his being able to call himself a friend of Nelson Mandela. The versatile cabaret artist is still fighting, in his own way, for the ideals of the democratic "rainbow society."

South Africans know this transvestite artist best from his role as Evita Bezuidenhout, the "Boer aunt." This fictitious character, garishly made-up in drag, uses wit and sarcasm to make fun of the everyday racism, devastating corruption, and political absurdities of South Africa under the dominance of the African National Congress. During performances in his theater, with its wild and glittering decorations, Uys banters with the numerous international visitors in the audience; he loves to mock the quirks of nations or world events in the manner of a stand-up comedian.

Uys founded his dinner theater in Darling's former railroad station. It contains studios and meeting rooms as well as a wonderfully chaotic shop. It is half museum, half retail store, crammed with books, pictures, arts and crafts, caricatures, posters, and documents testifying to Evita's enormous worldwide resonance.

For many years, "Tannie ('Auntie') Evita" has been an icon of modern South Africa. Uys, whose Jewish mother fled Nazi Germany, is still active in countless projects. More than a million schoolchildren have already listened to his lectures in schools on sex, contraception, and AIDS – hardly anyone seems more convincing than the man who was painfully ostracized from society for many years due to his convictions, his homosexuality, and his courage.

Address Old Darling Station, 8 Arcadia Street, Darling 7345, Tel +27/224922851, www.evita.co.za | **Getting there** By car: take N7 for 50 miles in the direction of Malmesbury; turn left on Philadelphia Road, right on R304, which becomes Dassenberg Road; continue on R307 to Darling | **Hours** Performances in the afternoons on Sat and Sun; restaurant open daily 10am–4pm | **Tip** Darling Olives Farm, about 2 miles outside of Darling toward Yzerfontein, offers olive products and picnics (baskets with freshly baked bread and delicacies) and, in the harvesting season (April–June), guided tours concerning the olive industry.

33 The Flea Market
Bargains galore in Milnerton

Cape Town has many exciting and lively markets. One of the most unusual is the flea market in Milnerton. Not far from the beach, and with a splendid view of Cape Town and Table Mountain, you can find both curious and practical things on weekends. The market is particularly popular with locals. Souvenirs typical of the country and African arts and crafts, normally very much in demand by tourists, play a secondary role here.

Instead, you can immerse yourself in the real life of the South Africans. With its 250 stands, the market reflects, in its way, the country's social disunity. Colonial antiques, old coins, books, and paintings are scattered among toys and dolls, bric-a-brac, silverware, and porcelain. But simple homemade chairs and cabinets are also offered, most of which probably end up in the huts of the sprawling townships. There are also piles of suspiciously cheap perfumes, batteries, and razor blades – all in their original packaging, as well as electronic parts, tools, cell phones, clothing, scarves knit by hand, hats, caps, and quirky fashion accessories.

The flea market is a field day for bargain hunters. The clientele is mainly made up of cunning natives who know that there are things to be found here for ridiculously low prices. If you would like to photograph the market, however, be careful not provoke the vendors. Some of them don't seem to like it when cameras are turned on them or their merchandise.

Bicycles are also repaired at the flea market, and small custom-made bookshelves or benches can be ordered. Finally, there are all kinds of stands with cakes, sandwiches, fried octopus, fatty South-African Boerewors sausages, and even home-brewed ginger beer.

Address Otto du Plessis Drive, Paarden Island, Milnerton, Cape Town 7435 | **Getting there** By car: take N1, exit 4, and turn onto county road R27, on the left after about 2 miles. By public transit: Bus T1, Zoarlei stop | **Hours** Sat and Sun 8am–2pm | **Tip** Milnerton Lagoon is a little lake with flamingos and pelicans, popular among windsurfers and sailors.

34_ The Flower Market
Fresh blooms for more than a century

The exact date when the flower market on Adderley Street between Strand and Darling Streets was opened can no longer be ascertained. Some say it was around 1900; others say ten years later. The street had already been named in 1850 after the Conservative British politician Charles Adderley (1814–1905), who had managed to put a stop to the plans of the British government at that time to turn Cape Town into a penal colony.

The flower stands out on the sidewalk of Adderley, Cape Town's main shopping thoroughfare, are harbingers of the market, located in a shopping arcade between tall commercial houses on Trafalgar Street. It is like an alleyway submerged in a rainbow of flowers. Tall steel trusswork supports corrugated roofing and illuminated globes, allowing daylight in around the edges and imparting the airy impression of a gallery.

The market is privately operated; the merchants, some of whom have been selling flowers for decades and are known for their friendly and playful banter, are licensed by the city and have to reapply for their stands at regular intervals. Mainly cut stems are sold, in all thinkable variations, and mostly at bargain prices. For more than a hundred years, their freshness has been maintained in the same manner: in basins constantly filled with water.

The colorful market is most crowded during the afternoon, when many business people quickly buy a few fresh blooms before leaving the inner city after work – around 5pm, after which the downtown area quite suddenly goes empty.

Particularly popular among the Capetonians are roses; lilies; and the protea, belonging to the fynbos group. The largest of these blooms is the king protea, South Africa's national flower, which can reach a diameter of up to a foot.

Address Trafalgar Street between Adderley and Parliament Streets, City, Cape Town 8000 | **Getting there** By public transit: Bus 102/103, 105–109, Darling Street stop; "Hop on-Hop off" bus, Long Street Tour Office stop | **Hours** Mon–Fri 8am–5pm (sometimes until 8pm on weekdays), Sat 8am–2pm | **Tip** Have a look at the Pan African Market at 76 Long Street and enjoy a cup of coffee there (8:30am–5:30pm). A part of the proceeds is given to families in the townships.

35 _ The Flying Archbishop
God bless your lunch

Since June 2014, an archbishop has been hovering over the tables of the renowned Savoy Cabbage restaurant. The installation, called *Arch*, by Ed Young, depicts Archbishop Desmond Tutu – the eloquent ally of Nelson Mandela in the struggle against the racist apartheid system, winner of the Nobel Peace Prize, and a Cape Town icon – in midair, holding on to a chandelier in the restaurant's dining room. The artist created the radiantly smiling dignitary on the occasion of the inauguration of the Cape Town branch of Idasa, the Institute for a Democratic Alternative in South Africa, in 2010.

Ed Young failed to win the artistic competition launched by Idasa with his draft of *Arch*, but the management of the Institute liked the idea nonetheless. They viewed Young's archbishop jubilantly grasping a crystal chandelier as a kind of sardonically laughing angel of vengeance symbolizing waste and luxury. The artist was asked to carry out the sculpture. An art critic interpreted the chandelier as a "symbol of the light of divine truth" urging Tutu to combat the corruption rife in South Africa.

Tutu himself attended the presentation of his life-size alter ego at Idasa's then-headquarters on Spin Street, and characteristically poked fun at the artist and his irreverent idea – admitting, however, that the work hit the nail on the head, and that Young had captured his personality: "Ceremonious, amused, but a bit threatening."

Idasa no longer exists, but the installation, owned by Richard Calland, a professor of law, found its way back to the public. The owners of the Savoy Cabbage enthusiastically accepted his offer to hang *Arch* in their high-ceilinged establishment. It is in good company among other contemporary works of art that often appear along the restaurant's brick walls.

Address Savoy Cabbage Restaurant & Champagne Bar, 101 Hout Street, City, Cape Town 8000, Tel. +27/214242626, www.savoycabbage.co.za | **Getting there** By public transit: Bus 105, Strand Street stop; "Hop on-Hop off" bus, Long Street Tour Office stop | **Hours** Mon–Fri 12–14:30pm and 7–10:30pm, Sat 7–10:30pm | **Tip** The Dutch Lutheran Church, the oldest Lutheran Church in South Africa, was originally founded in a warehouse on Strand Street near Buitengracht during a time of repression; the structure has been renovated numerous times.

36 — The Freemason Temple
Architectural jewel behind Parliament

Goede Hoop Lodge is a gem of early Cape Dutch architecture, inside and out. But it's not easy to access. As the building is located behind a parking lot right next to Parliament, you have to go through security checks to gain entry, and there is no admittance without registration. Consecrated in 1803, it is the oldest Masonic temple still in existence in Africa. Although the building burned down almost to its foundations in 1892, it was faithfully reconstructed.

In the middle of the building, you can marvel at the splendid temple room, with its altar, flags, thrones, benches, and sword stands. It seats far more than a hundred Freemasons. The wings lead to gloomy vaults and secluded chambers. You can examine mysterious ornaments, artistic statues, sculptures, paintings and portraits throughout the temple.

The history of South Africa's Freemasons is not without controversy. Though members emphasize their rejection of discrimination – "Freemasonry unites men with high ideals, regardless of their color, their religion, or their worldly status," from the beginning, through apartheid, and for many years beyond, there was not a single black person belonging to the lodge. A special regulation was passed in the 1970s allowing members of mixed ethnic descent. The first black South African was not welcomed until 2007, however. South Africa's Freemasons deny the age-old rumor that Nelson Mandela was a member. Female membership is prohibited to this day.

Entrepreneur, pioneer, and colonial politician Cecil Rhodes, who played a pivotal role in the shaping and formation of southern Africa at the end of the 19th century, was a Freemason and attended the temple of this secretive lodge committed to the ideals of humanitarianism and freedom.

Address 1 Bouquet Street, City, Cape Town 8000 | **Getting there** By public transit: Bus 103, Roeland Street stop; "Hop on-Hop off" bus, St. George's Cathedral stop | **Hours** Reservations required to visit, guided tours once or twice a month; reservations made through the Grand Lodge Secretariat: Tel +27/214615400 (Mon, Wed, Fri 9am–12pm) | **Tip** Close by, on Church Square, stands a monument to Jan Hendrik Hofmeyr (1845–1909), cofounder of the "Afrikaner Bond," a national-conservative political organization that succeeded in making Afrikaans an official language next to English in 1925.

37 — The Fugard Theatre
Modern stage against racism

South Africa's most famous playwright, Athol Fugard, had to be persuaded to lend his name to the theater in historic District Six. But since its opening in 2010 – with the help of some affluent admirers of Fugard – the theater, located in a former clothing warehouse and a neo-Gothic church, has been close to the writer's heart. For it is from this quarter that the government brutally displaced more than 60,000 black inhabitants in 1966 – declaring it a "white quarter" – and that this impassioned critic of the racist apartheid regime now finds a stage for his message of freedom and equality.

Today, the 335-seat theater often presents contemporary dramas concerning the struggle for democracy and human rights as well as such popular musicals as *The Rocky Horror Picture Show* and *Cabaret*.

Frequently, the theater also puts on Fugard's own plays, sometimes directed by the playwright himself. Now and then he even performs, as in the 2014 production of his two-person play *The Shadow of the Hummingbird*, in which he dealt impressively with the themes of age, infirmity, and death. The piece was based on his own diaries.

Now based in California, where he is an adjunct professor at the University of California San Diego, Fugard primarily explores the most controversial subjects of his South African homeland in his works: racial relationships, the prejudices of whites and blacks, pervasive violence, brutalization through poverty, and the search for the meaning of life.

During the winter season on Sundays at 11am, broadcasts of major opera and ballet performances in London or New York can be viewed in high resolution on a movie screen in the Fugard's auditorium.

Address Caledon and Harrington Streets, District Six, City, Cape Town 8001, Tel +27/214614554, www.thefugard.com | **Getting there** By public transit: Bus 103, Lower Buitenkant stop; "Hop on-Hop off" bus, The Castle of Good Hope stop | **Hours** Performances start at 8pm | **Tip** A popular place to meet before and after the performances – for the theater crew and cast as well as the audience – is the nearby Dias Tavern, at 15 Caledon Street.

38 __ The Gallery Crawl
Treasure trove for art lovers

The Capetonians are justly proud of their many-faceted culture, and of the creativity of their artists. One sign of this is the uniquely broad scope of the more than 100 art galleries scattered across the city, with concentrations mainly in the Woodstock and Observatory quarters – as well as on picturesque Church Street and its side streets in the heart of Cape Town. Here, you can find the works of such renowned South African artists as Simon Jonaes, Peter van Straten, Anthony Gadd, and Vaness Berlein.

The emphasis is on contemporary art from South Africa and the neighboring states. Some galleries specialize in ceramics, sculpture, or prints, and offer frequently changing exhibitions. Worldart, for instance, displays the work of nine South African artists per month – alongside longer-term exhibits of famous national artists.

The Association for Visual Arts (AVA) is a nonprofit gallery showing mainly modern art. The works are often sold to the highest bidder at auctions that are quite lively and fun; you can sometimes buy high-quality pictures, sculpture, and ceramics for astoundingly low prices.

The Erdmann Contemporary gallery has become especially well known for exhibitions of local comic illustrators and artistic photographers. The Cape Gallery, on the other hand, concentrates on traditional South-African landscape paintings. The realism of these works demonstrates the artistic orientation of many 19th-century artists, who tried to paint as true to life as possible.

G2 Art focuses above all on contemporary work, and includes a lot of sculpture and photography. You can also find copies of historic photos of Cape Town here, some of which are more than 100 years old.

Address Cape Gallery, 60 Church Street, City, Cape Town 8000, www.first-thursdays.co.za | **Getting there** By public transit: Bus 101, Church Street stop; "Hop on-Hop off" bus, Long Street Tour Office stop | **Hours** Mon–Fri 9am–6pm, Sat 9am–3pm (some galleries are also open on Sundays); the galleries are open until 9pm on every first Thursday of the month | **Tip** The artist Siphiwe Ngwenya uses houses in townships to stage exhibitions and offers tours through the Maboneng Township Arts Experience (Tel +27/218241773, www.maboneng.com).

39 The Gandhi Monument
Meet the great Indian leader at the University

In November 2008, a bust of Mahatma Gandhi (1869–1948), created by the Indian artist Gautam Pal, was ceremoniously unveiled at the University of the Western Cape (UWC). The work was a gift of the Indian government. This act was meant to honor both the great Indian leader, who spent a very significant portion of his life in South Africa, and the university, which was an active bulwark against racism and apartheid for many years.

Gandhi came to South Africa in 1884 as a young lawyer, and was politically active in the region for the following two decades. He particularly fought for the rights of some 60,000 Asian Indians living in South Africa, who were greatly suffering from discrimination by the British and the Boers. During his years in South Africa and in the resistance against increasingly harassing laws issued by the government, Gandhi developed his philosophy of nonviolent disobedience, called *satyagraha*, which finally led to India's liberation from British rule after his return to his homeland.

The university was founded in 1959 during apartheid as a school of higher education for ostracized mixed race students, who were no longer being admitted to "white" universities.

The UWC received its first black president in 1975; its students protested openly against apartheid starting in 1982. With its 15,000 students in seven colleges, the university also operates the Mayibuye Centre for History and Culture – which houses the most comprehensive archive in South Africa chronicling its history of suppression, discrimination, and apartheid, and is also associated with the Robben Island Museum. The center documents student resistance against the regime and its ideology.

Address University of the Western Cape (UWC), Robert Sobukwe Road, Bellville, Cape Town 7535, Tel. +27/219592911, www.uwc.ac.za | **Getting there** By car: take N2, turn before the airport onto M10, which leads to Robert Sobukwe Road. By public transit: Metrorail blue line, Unibell Station | **Tip** There is another impressive statue of Gandhi in front of the entrance to the Mount Nelson Hotel on Orange Street in the inner city. At UWC, there is also a bust of former archbishop Desmond Tutu.

40 — The Grand Café

Relaxing on the beach

The Grand Café is *the* beach restaurant in Cape Town, although Schimmy's Beach Club at the Waterfront is actually quite similar. Maybe the Grand Café isn't one of the very best culinary destinations in town, but its African and French cuisine is nothing to sneeze at. The drinks are first class, and the location is one of a kind: right on the Waterfront and close to Green Point Stadium, with a panorama of the open sea and the ships gliding by in front of you, and Table Mountain and Signal Hill behind you. The Grand Café is a refuge for high-level relaxation. Sitting on the sandy beach beneath a white parasol with a good drink will put you into quite an idiosyncratic mood. Somehow, it's as though the city were suddenly a long way off.

There had been a beach bar here for many years – a bit run-down, with erratic opening hours. In 2009, a consortium of restaurateurs took over the location and spruced it up. The former wharf warehouse was elaborately converted, equipped with a 50-foot bar and a lounge, and extended by a gift shop where a large collection of Panama hats can be perused.

But the highlight is the beach. On a big wooden terrace reached by boardwalks stand tables for those who prefer to dine right next to the water. Distributed in the sand with plenty of space are groups of seats, cozy deck chairs, and comfortable armchairs. Drinks are mixed at both beach bars while you dig your feet in the sand. The area, however, isn't suitable for swimming.

Here, at Granger Bay, there is an intimation of the Côte d'Azur. The Capetonians like to bring their out-of-town visitors to the Grand Café and thus surprise them. Tourists prefer to cavort on the Waterfront close by. The Grand Café is often booked for events, for you can party here – very well, and undisturbed.

Address Grand Café, Haul Road (Granger Bay), Green Point, Cape Town 8005, Tel +27/214250551, www.grandafrica.com | **Getting there** By car: take Granger Boulevard and then Haol Road up to the parking lot. By public transit: Bus 104, Somerset Hospital or Breakwater stop | **Hours** Tue–Sat 12pm–11pm, Sun lunch, closed June 30–July 31 | **Tip** There is another Grand Café in Camps Bay, at 35 Victoria Road. And just ten feet away, you'll run into the hip Café Caprice.

41 The Grand Daddy
Spend the night on the roof

If you're young and adventurous, and you like to party but don't want to stay in Cape Town's backpacker-filled hostels, the Grand Daddy could be the ideal place for you. In many respects, this four-star hotel is garish and offbeat. If you take your evening drink in the Sky Bar on the roof terrace under an open Bedouin tent, you'll find yourself among mostly young guests who often love to hear loud, booming music. But you can also reside on the roof: seven differently and fantastically decorated trailers offer some of the most original accommodations in town. Young artists and interior decorators have furbished the camping wagons according to various themes such as "Afro Funk" or "The Wizard of Oz." Little garden fences, red mailboxes, and plants emphasize each campsite's character.

Out of his love for experimentation, the hotel's manager ordered the classic Airstream trailers from the United States in 2008. They were then hoisted up with a crane to the top of the building. In this way, a unique atmosphere was created on the roof – from where one can watch the action of turbulent Long Street against the backdrop of Table Mountain and the downtown high-rises – which visibly animates the guests to party and dance.

On Mondays, the roof turns into the "Pink Flamingo Open Air Cinema" with 32 seats. Such old and new classics as *Casablanca* or *Pretty Woman* are screened. The four-story house on the corner also has 26 normal, comfortable, color-splashed rooms as well as the Daddy Cool Bar, with its slight red-light-district flair, the L'Apero Restaurant, and a 19th-century elevator, the oldest one in town. Back in 1895, the Hotel Metropole stood here at the beginning of Long Street; it became a landmark of the "Mother City." The name "Grand Daddy" is an allusion to this nickname for Cape Town.

Address Grand Daddy Hotel, 38 Long Street, City, Cape Town 8000, Tel +27/214247247, www.granddaddy.co.za | **Getting there** By public transit: Bus 101, Mid Long Street stop; "Hop on-Hop off" bus, Long Street Tour Office stop | **Hours** Sky Bar: Mon 4:30–6:30pm, Tue–Sat 4:30–9:30pm | **Tip** The Mama Africa on Long Street is a classic restaurant and music bar. There is live African music every day except Sunday.

42 The GrandWest Casino
The palace of diversions

"GrandWest" lays claim to being South Africa's biggest casino. On average, every day, about 18,000 people visit this stronghold of amusement, with its facade of stone columns and marble reminiscent of old colonial buildings. The broad scope and types of offerings in this "Wonderland around the Clock" just outside of Cape Town convey an inkling of Las Vegas. In the gambling halls and the adjoining salons, there are tables for all of the customary games from roulette to poker, as well as 2,500 slot machines. Owned by the hotel chain Sun International, GrandWest also aims to be attractive to families and guests with little interest in gambling.

Most unusual for Africa, the casino building complex includes an Olympic-size skating rink. On 100 by 200 feet of ice, more than 100 skaters can glide around at the same time without getting too much in one another's way. Skates are available to rent.

GrandWest also has a five-star hotel, concert halls, theaters, meeting rooms, movie theaters, a discotheque, a bowling alley, and, of course, numerous restaurants, bars, and nightclubs. International pop stars, musicians, wrestlers, and boxers appear here frequently.

Surprising for European visitors is the extensive offering of games for children, who are lured into a colorfully decorated gaming hall containing a small go-cart track, auto scooters, a carousel, a big adventure playground in a "magic fortress," and all kinds of games of skill. In the "magic arcade" are rows of video games and machines ostensibly suitable for children; most of these work with plastic money, with which one can win material prizes. Whoever wants to become a "gambler" can get an early start here.

Address 1 Vanguard Drive, Goodwood, Cape Town 7460, Tel +27/215057777, www.grandwest@suninternational.com | **Getting there** By car: take N2 in the direction of Somerset West, exit 11 (M17 Pinelands, Epping), turn left onto M16 toward Epping and Goodwood. By public transit: Metrorail Green Line, Goodwood Station | **Hours** 24 hours a day | **Tip** The Hanover Street Jazz Club in the GrandWest building complex is designed in the style of New Orleans in the 1920s and offers high-quality jazz on two floors (opens at 9pm).

43 The Gravestone
The garden of extinct plants

There are only a few corners of the globe with as rich a spectrum of plants as the rainy Cape region with its moderate temperatures. Founded in 1913, Kirstenbosch claims to have been the first botanical garden in the world to commit itself primarily to the conservation of regional flora. Domestic plants are dominant among the 700 varieties found on the 1300-acre area on the eastern slope of Table Mountain.

An inconspicuous and unique monument is a reminder, however, of how many species no longer exist: the weighty, flat gravestone in the "Garden of Extinction" is dedicated – as a representative of all species that have died out – to Erica pyramidalis, a kind of heather that hasn't existed here since 1907. The rapid settlement of the Cape crowded out the original colorful mixture of fynbos vegetation at the time.

In the carefully cultivated beds around the gravestone, there are nearly 1,500 plants threatened with extinction today. Along the small loop road through the endangered flora, signs in front of the plants inform the visitor about each species, explaining where and why it is in danger, and what is being done to protect it.

Here, there also grows a relative of the heather mourned on the gravestone – Erica verticillata – apparently saved and revitalized by botanists at the last moment.

Visiting this extraordinary garden is definitely worthwhile – but those who take a walk through the 89 acres of these exquisite, vast grounds should familiarize themselves with the layout and points of interest beforehand. Without a map and a chart, the centuries-old trees, the Xhosa hut with herbs for natural medicine, and the protective hedge of wild almond trees (put up against the bushmen in 1660) are hard to find.

Address Botanical Gardens, Rhodes Drive, Newlands, Cape Town 7735, Tel +27/217998783, www.sanbi.org/gardens/kirstenbosch | **Getting there** By car: take M3, Kirstenbosch exit. By public transit: Golden Arrow bus, Mowbray-Kitsenbosch route, Kirstenbosch stop; "Hop on-Hop off" bus, Kirstenbosch stop | **Hours** Sept–March, daily 8am–7pm, April–Aug, daily 8am–6pm; volunteer guides offer tours Mon–Sat | **Tip** Between November and April, all kinds of concerts take place late every Sunday afternoon on the open-air stage in Kirstenbosch, including performances by local pop stars, jazz groups, and classical musicians.

44 Heritage Square
A block full of surprises

Thanks to the efforts of Cape Town's architects, monument protectors, and numerous influential citizens, the buildings on the square block bordered by Buitengracht, Hout, Shortmarket, and Bree Streets are still standing. That this complex shines with new brilliance today is due to the Cape Town Heritage Trust, an independent nonprofit organization that was founded in 1987 to preserve Cape Town's architectural and cultural heritage and re-enliven the inner city.

In the mid-1980s, the city government decided to demolish the tawdry block at Riebeeck Square with its run-down town houses from the 18th and 19th centuries, in order to construct a new expressway. A gigantic garage for 2,000 vehicles was planned for the location, which was vociferously protested. Originally built in 1771, the block, with its picturesque residential houses and its charming interior courtyard, was eventually handed over to Cape Town Heritage Trust, which thoroughly restored it, starting in the mid-1990s, and finally gave it the name Heritage Square.

Gazing into Heritage Square takes you on a trip back to 18th-century Cape Town. But the block, with its faithfully restored Cape Dutch and Georgian facades, offers much more: excellent restaurants, art galleries, a film studio, a blacksmith's, and the Cape Heritage Hotel, which is integrated into an edifice built in 1780.

Spend some time ambling through the hotel lobby's gallery of photos, which chronicle the history of Heritage Square, before visiting the quaint inner courtyard. There you can sit down at a table of any of six restaurants, far from the hectic rush of the city – ostensibly under Cape Town's oldest grapevine, which was planted here in 1781.

Address Heritage Square, 90 Bree Street, City, Cape Town 8000 | **Getting there** By public transit: Bus 101, Longmarket Street stop, or Bus 105, Strand Street stop; "Hop on-Hop off" bus, Long Street stop | **Hours** Hotel, restaurant, and business hours, usually 11am–11pm daily | **Tip** Just a few steps away is Greenmarket Square, one of the liveliest souvenir markets in town.

45 _ The Imhoff Farm
Three dozen stores under one roof

On the way to the Cape, via the villages Kommetjie and Scarborough, you'll be surprised by the sight of camels resting in a meadow at the edge of the road, waiting for customers. And if you look more closely, you'll discover these "ships of the desert" are just one of numerous attractions at the expansive Imhoff Farm. Crossing the grounds you'll reach a gigantic corral with some 40 horses, which are part of the core business of the country estate.

The farm has a turbulent history that began with the Dutch East India Company. In order to provide a safe harbor to protect their ships from the dangerous winter storms, Governor Gustaaf Willem van Imhoff initiated the construction of the harbor with docks where Simon's Town, named after first cape governor Simon van der Stel, is situated today. Van Imhoff had a warehouse built and, in 1743, a farm constructed in nearby Noordhoek to supply the ships with provisions.

Since 1912, Imhoff Farm has been owned by the Van der Horst family. Though devastated by fire in 1958, much of the farm was rebuilt true to the original design. For more than 25 years it has operated as a family-friendly farmstead that's open to the public, offering visitors a variety of activities and amenities. Rides through the ever-changing landscape, especially along the miles of dune beach from nearby Noordhoek, are extraordinarily charming.

There are some 30 stores – most of them operated by the owners, and craftspeople – among them a cheese maker, a chocolatier, a pottery shop, a wine merchant, and a barber. There's even a snake farm! The whole estate is rounded off by three restaurants, one of which, the Blue Water Cafe, has a lovely view of the Wildevoel Vlei and its little lake.

Address Kommetjie Road, Kommetjie, Cape Town 7975, Tel +27/217834545, www.imhofffarm.co.za | **Getting there** By car: take M3, then M64 and M65; you can also arrive via Chapman's Peak Drive through Noordhoek | **Hours** Daily 9am–5pm; horse rides: Mon–Sat, three rides daily, Tel +27/827741191; camel rides: Tue–Sun 12–4pm, reservations necessary for long rides, Tel +27/217891711 | **Tip** Not far from Imhoff Farm lies Noordhoek Farm Village, with a similar concept.

46 — The Irma Stern Museum
The great artist's eccentric lifestyle

In Cape Town during the 1940s and 1950s, an invitation to dinner at the home of the somewhat eccentric artist Irma Stern was much sought after. Even back then, an evening in the domicile of the infamous chain-smoker in the Rosebank District was almost like a visit to a museum, as the most famous South-African Expressionist painter filled the interior of her externally rather nondescript house not only with her own works, but also with those of other artists.

A long dark table, whittled chairs, painted cupboards, and lots of red satin in the dining room give the visitor an idea of the imposing, somewhat fustian atmosphere that must have reigned here during those famous dinners. A few years after Stern's death in 1966, the house became a museum in earnest. The picturesque studio of the willful painter remains in its original condition, with its many African sculptures and textiles documenting Africa's influence on her work.

A daughter of German-Jewish immigrants, Stern studied at the Academy of the Arts in Weimar, Germany. In 1926, after a number of successes in Europe, she returned to Cape Town and lived in Rosebank for almost four decades. She was one of the few South-African artists to win international acclaim. In 2011, one of her works was sold for the equivalent of 3 million euros.

Stern was proud of the versatility of her work, which encompassed oil and watercolor paintings and drawings. For her, everything became an object for artistic elaboration: furniture, doors, windows, walls. She decorated her home with countless antiques, African artifacts, Oriental art, doors imported from Zanzibar, and precious European furniture.

On the second floor of the museum, there is a gallery with works of contemporary art offered for sale.

Address Cecil Road, Rosebank, Cape Town 7700, Tel +27/216855686, www.irmastern.co.za | **Getting there** By car: take N2, Rhodes Avenue exit (6D), and turn right on Cecil Road; By public transit: Metrorail Red Line, Rosebank station | **Hours** Tue–Fri 10am–5pm, Sat 10am–2pm | **Tip** Mostert's Mill, built in 1796, located directly on the M3 expressway, is the only windmill in Africa south of the Sahara still in operation (reservations to view are required: "Friends of Mostert's Mill," Rhodes Avenue, Mowbray, Cape Town 7975, Tel +27/217821305).

47 — The Khayelitsha Shopping Center
Shopping in the Cape Flats

Not all of the townships are slums today, but many millions of extremely impoverished blacks and mixed-race South Africans still live in them. Before 1994, the apartheid regime forced nearly all non-whites into such settlements, with miserable living conditions – usually on the edges of the big cities: in Cape Town, in the so-called Cape Flats. Today, that has partly changed due to a number of municipal construction projects, a growing supply of corrugated iron shacks with water and electricity, and an enormously high social budget. Some townships have developed into acceptable, occasionally even attractive residential districts. Khayelitsha, Cape Town's biggest township, hasn't gotten that far yet. But change in this settlement with a population of millions, infamous for poverty and violence, is visibly documented by the shopping center at its edge, opened in 2005 as the first mall in a township in the province.

Though tourists can shop safely in the mall's more or less 40 stores, there is none of the luxury and abundance that distinguish some other commercial centers in Cape Town. All of South Africa's biggest chains have outlets here, and the large banks have branches. The rather modest assortment of merchandise is addressed mainly to customers who often earn less than the equivalent of 100 euros a month. There are also offices of social authorities and of the police, as well as a local court, and security personnel and surveillance cameras are everywhere.

If you visit this mall, you will be confronted by South Africa's social realities – whereby all manner of miracle healers, political activists, legal advisers, lottery vendors, and fortune-tellers, bring in some variety and color.

Address Walter Sisulu and Steve Biko Roads, Khayelitsha, Cape Town 7784 | **Getting there** Going by car is recommended, preferably in small groups or organized tours; coming from Cape Town, take M2 in the direction of Somerset West, Walter Sisulu Road (M 45) exit | **Hours** Mon–Sat 9am–5pm | **Tip** The Khayelitsha Museum in the Mandela Park District shows the history of the township and its mainly Xhosa population (open Mon–Fri 9am–4pm, Sat and Sun 10am–noon).

48 The Labour Museum
The history of revolts and strikes

This simple museum building in the township of Lwandle is itself suggestive of the desolate situation of the itinerant and guest laborers in South Africa during apartheid. Inside the museum, which opened in 2000, everyday objects, papers, photos, and drawings document the horrifying fate of millions of human beings who had to live and slave under the most wretched conditions imaginable. A true-to-life hostel for six black workers is a part of the museum. Some of the workers came from as far away as Zimbabwe, Malawi, and Lesotho, for even extremely poorly paid work was mainly available in the white metropolitan areas around the mines and industrial complexes. The white rulers crammed them into the cramped barracks and shacks of the townships.

It was mostly men who worked for next to nothing, separated by great distances from their families. The women, who were needed mostly in households, kitchens, and in the tourism sector, lived apart from the men. Breaking out of this fate was extremely difficult, not only because there were no other prospects for work or earning money, but also because the apartheid regime had limited the blacks' freedom to travel through the use of strict identity-card regulations, the so-called "reference books." Anger over such harassments frequently unleashed vehement protests.

The Lwandle Migrant Labour Museum was awarded a prize as the best museum in the province in 2009. Photomontages, artistic photographs, and installations by South-African artists deal with the subjects of homeland and displacement. The collection of photos, *Transported of KwaNdebele*, by South-African photographer David Goldblatt, is considered the museum's most valuable exhibition. There are regular showings of films that provide bone-chilling testimony of everyday life during predemocratic times.

Address Lwandle Migrant Labour Museum, Old Community Hall, Vulindlela Street, Lwandle, Cape Town 7140, Tel +27/218456119, www.lwandle.com | **Getting there** By car: take N2 to Somerset West, Broadlands Drive exit, take the first right turn, and then stay on the left on Nunqubela Street; take left turns at the next two intersections | **Hours** Mon–Fri 8am–4pm | **Tip** Not far from the Labour Museum, on Mondeor Road, you'll find the outdoor animal enclosure called Monkey Town (Somerset West, Tel +27/218581060, www.monkeys.co.za).

49 Langa Cultural Center
Art and music in the township

The Guga S'Thebe Art and Cultural Centre is more than a community resource. It is an important educational center for the many young unemployed in Langa; but it's also an architecturally distinctive building complex featuring frescos, mosaics, and sculptures, and has received several awards for its design. This municipal facility has skillfully bundled a variety of facilities and offerings: a tourism office, social counseling, art workshops, music and dance lessons, and courses for ceramicists, locksmiths, and cabinet makers. The amphitheater and various halls house a children's theater and host concerts, conferences, and political meetings.

In the Xhosa language, *guga s'thebe* means "aging plate." This is an allusion to the traditional serving platter around which everyone in the house assembles. The center opened in 1999 to "encourage Langa's inhabitants to take the reigns of responsibility," the local guides emphasize. Tours through Langa are available to visitors, who are thus confronted by the realities of everyday life in this deprived area.

Langa, Cape Town's oldest township, was built in 1927 as the first large and contiguous living area for cheap labor. Located near the city, it was, from the point of view of security personnel, easily accessible and thus easily controllable. Monuments and works of art draw attention to the population's long struggle for democratic rights. The community's refusal to be vanquished by poverty is evidenced by the beautiful pictures and sculptures they brought into the gloom of their barracks and corrugated metal shacks.

When Cape Town was the design capital of the world in 2014, Langa became a part of the Maboneng Township Arts Experience. Since then, art exhibitions can be visited in private houses in Langa.

Address Guga S'Thebe Art and Cultural Centre, Washington Street, Langa, Cape Town 7455 | **Getting there** By car: take N 2 (Nelson Mandela Boulevard), stay to the left on M 2, exit 12 (Bhunga Avenue), take the third street to the right onto Washington Street. By public transit: Golden Arrow bus, Cape Town-Village 3 and Village 3-Langa route; Metrorail blue line, Langa Station | **Hours** Mon – Fri 8am – 4:30pm, Sat and Sun 8am – 2pm | **Tip** The unusual Monument to the March of the 30,000, at Washington Square, commemorates the protests of the blacks in Langa against the Sharpeville massacre on March 30, 1960 (a third of a mile away from the cultural center).

50 The Leopard
How the big cat got on the rock

Hardly anyone knows anymore today that the Cape peninsula was inhabited by carnivores – even leopards – less than a century ago. But hunters and poachers were always after the shy, proud animals. The last leopard is supposed to have been shot in 1930 near Hout Bay; others say that the final remaining member of the species was spotted in 1937 at Little Lion's Head. However this may be, in memory of the exterminated leopards and other wild animals in the Cape region, a gigantic figure of a leopard was installed at the end of Hout Bay Beach in 1963 on a steeply towering rock.

Sponsored by a big beverage group, the bronze statue weighing 650 pounds was conceived and created by the South-African sculptor and author Ivan Mitford-Barberton (1896–1976), who lived in Hout Bay. (His ancestors were among the first British settlers to arrive in South Africa in 1820.) Mitford-Barberton had studied in London under the famous sculptor Henry Moore and in 1927 returned to South Africa, where he opened an atelier in Hout Bay. In the 1930s he designed the spectacular facade of the Mutual Heights Building in Cape Town; at nearly 300 feet, it was the highest building in Africa at the time.

The artist had been contemplating modeling a leopard for more than 20 years by the time the project was carried out in the early 1960s; his first sketches go back to the end of the 1930s. The bronze statue was heaved up to its current location between the rock and the tread in an airy strut construction made of wood and bamboo and firmly anchored there.

If you drive past the leopard and see it out of the corner of your eye, you can't help but wonder: How did it get there? And why a leopard, of all things? Now, you know.

Address Hout Bay, Cape Town 7806 (at the end of Hout Bay Beach in the direction of Noordhoek) | **Getting there** By car: take the M6 exit from Hout Bay to Chapman's Peak on the right-hand side | **Tip** The Hout Bay Museum on Andrews Road is full of fascinating history; it also displays documentation of the construction of Chapman's Peak Drive.

51 The Lighthouse
The seamark at Green Point

The Green Point lighthouse – the very first on the South-African coast – was built in 1824 by Hermann Schütte (1761–1844). Schütte arrived in Cape Town from Bremen, Germany, in 1790, gained a foothold here, and spent the rest of his life as a master builder and sculptor. While working as a stonecutter for the Dutch East India Company he was severely wounded in an explosives accident in the Robben Island quarry, resulting in his release from service. From that time on, he worked as a freelance architect and exercised great influence on Cape Town's construction activities. He received the commission to build the fortified lighthouse at Green Point from the governor.

Schütte built a square-shaped tower using massive masonry walls sporting red and white diagonal lines. It is now a national monument. Originally operated with sperm-whale oil and petroleum, the tower's signals were visible some four nautical miles away. In 1865, the lighthouse was heightened from its original 52.5 feet to its present 65.5 feet. It received a new-fashioned foghorn in 1926 and was electrified three years later. The light of the tower thus became visible for up to 25 nautical miles, enabling it to more successfully warn ships away from the rocky coastline. The lighthouse still functions today, flashing every ten seconds.

The district of Green Point, situated along Main Road, was an amusement quarter for whites during apartheid; but with the establishment of the waterfront complex and its attractions, many businesses in Green Point closed and some of them skidded down into the red-light milieu. Thanks especially to the soccer world championship in 2010 and the building of the new stadium, Green Point experienced a renaissance, and now has a lively bar and restaurant scene in addition to its many green areas.

Address Green Point Lighthouse, 100 Beach Road, Mouille Point, Cape Town 8005, Tel +27/214495172 and +27/217809232 | **Getting there** By public transit: Bus 104, Lighthouse stop; "Hop on-Hop off" bus, Green Point and Urban Park stop | **Hours** Year-round, Mon–Fri 10am–3pm | **Tip** A second municipal lighthouse, built in 1960, stands on Woodbridge Island in the suburb of Milnerton.

52 — The Lion Compound
Wild animals in Vredenheim

The white lions at Vredenheim Wine Farm are fascinating: supple and majestic, the mighty carnivores pace back and forth behind the high barred fences. However, the sight of the confined cats in such proximity to their natural habitat might strike some as strange. There used to be lions on the Cape. The keepers emphasize, however, that white lions, especially when young, are particularly endangered in the wild due to their conspicuous fur, and often fail to survive. In the open-air compounds of the Big Cat Park in Vredenheim, wild animals – leopards and tigers as well as lions – are obviously well taken care of; they also have much more space than their relatives in conventional zoos.

With its Big Cat Park, and its ostriches, zebras, and kudus running around in freedom, 321-year-old Vredenheim Wine Farm aims to distinguish itself from the many other lovely wine farms surrounding Stellenbosch. The beautiful estate, with its little lake and well-tended restaurant called Barrique – boasting tables on its veranda against the picturesque backdrop of the Helderberg Mountains – is also worth a visit. The farm offers not only wines that have won several prizes, but also various kinds of beer that it brews itself.

Vredenheim is one of the oldest estates in Stellenbosch; the earliest drawing of a Stellenbosch home appeared on a deed dated 1686 for the farm "Vredenburgh." In 1691, the first governor of the Dutch Cape colony, Simon van der Stel, formally granted the property to merchant and entrepreneur Hendrik Elbertz, from Osnabrück. The long main building still standing today was built in 1798 in the classic Cape Dutch style. It is now a listed edifice. The Bezuidenhout family, on the Cape for generations, has owned the estate since 1986.

Address Vredenheim Wine Farm, Stellenbosch 7600, Tel +27/218813878, www.vredenheim.co.za | **Getting there** By car: take the N2 expressway in the direction of Stellenbosch, Baden-Powell exit (county road R310) in the direction of Stellenbosch; drive 6 miles to Vredenheim | **Hours** Mon–Fri 9am–5pm, Sat and Sun 10am–3pm | **Tip** Nearby Boschendal Wine Farm is famous for its lovely park and big picnic baskets (Boschendal Wine Farm, exit from county road R310 into Pniel Road, Tel +27/218704274).

53 — The Marble Staircase
Where the end of apartheid began

On February 11, 1990, Nelson Mandela was released after being imprisoned for 27 years on Robben Island and in other jails. That day marked the beginning of a new chapter in South Africa's history: the irrevocable demise of the apartheid regime. The end of segregation had been ushered in by the longtime worldwide boycott of South Africa, and by growing unrest within the country, which had reached massive proportions. The decision to free Mandela was made by Frederik Willem de Klerk, the president at that time. De Klerk and Mandela went on to work cooperatively to create a multiracial democracy. Together, they received the Nobel Peace Prize in 1993.

The day Mandela was liberated, 100,000 people assembled at Grand Parade, the former drill ground – a marketplace today. They had been waiting for this extraordinary moment for hours, mad with joy and excitement; the atmosphere was vibrant, as it would be every time this hero of freedom appeared in public in subsequent years. Nelson Mandela; Winnie, his wife at the time; and his comrades-in-arms of the African National Congress (ANC) ascended the marble staircase of City Hall. Amidst the jubilation of the crowd, Mandela delivered his famous Liberty Address, beginning with the words, *"Amandla! i-Africa, mayibuye!"* (Power to the people! Africa is ours!). Four years later, Nelson Mandela became South Africa's first black president.

Cape Town City Hall – which was built in 1905 in the style of the Italian Renaissance, with its clock tower alluding to Big Ben in London – lost its function as a governmental seat in 1979, when the municipal executives and the administration moved to the Civic Centre, close by. Today, the historic building harbors the concert hall of the Cape Philharmonic Orchestra.

Address City Hall, Darling Street, City, Cape Town 8001 | **Getting there** By public transit: Bus 102/103, Darling Street stop; "Hop on-Hop off" bus, the Castle of Good Hope stop | **Hours** The interior of City Hall can be seen only in the context of special events hosted there | **Tip** The Cape Philharmonic Orchestra gives regular concerts in City Hall's Great Concert Hall. Twice a week, a market is held on Grand Parade.

54 The Maritime Centre
Noteworthy information on South-African seafaring

This rather nondescript museum on the upper floor of the Union-Castle House, built in 1919 in the old part of the harbor, imparts valuable insights into Cape Town's maritime history from the 17th to the 20th centuries. It shows the influence of the harbor on the development of the city and its inhabitants, and the man-made modifications to Table Bay.

Up until the middle of the 19th century, Cape Town had only a provisory harbor; the high-water mark still reached all the way up to the Castle of Good Hope. As most of the ships lay at anchor farther out in the ocean, they were exposed to severe storms and tempests. When Lloyds of London stopped insuring Cape Town ships wintering in Table Bay, the construction of a sturdy harbor with a massive breakwater was decided on. Today, Cape Town handles more than 11 million tons of freight annually, making it South Africa's third-largest industrial location. In 1988, Transnet Ltd. began converting the original basin into the Victoria and Albert Waterfront.

In the Maritime Centre, one finds a scale model of the Table Bay Harbor built in 1885 by the inmates of Breakwater Prison. You can also see numerous large models of ships of the Union-Castle Line, the subsequent mail line between London and Cape Town. Major ship catastrophes and shipwrecks all around Cape Town are illustrated.

A focal point of the exhibit is the impressive picture collection of the John H. Marsh Maritime Research Centre, comprising 20,000 photographs and showing ships from the 1920s to the 1960s. The Marsh Collection has registered, listed, and described 9,000 ships in detail. Another part of the Maritime Centre is a library with an archive of old logbooks, nautical maps, and ship registers.

Address Union-Castle House, Dock Road, V&A Waterfront, second floor, Cape Town 8000, Tel +27/214052880, www.iziko.org.za/museums/maritime-centre | **Getting there** Public transit: Bus 104, Nobel Square stop; "Hop on-Hop off" bus, Aquarium or Clock Tower stop | **Hours** Mon–Sun 10am–5pm | **Tip** You can take a harbor tour starting at the V&A Waterfront.

55   M'hudi
The first black-owned wine vineyard in South Africa

For Diale Rangaka, his wine farm is an adventure, a risky experiment. The former professor of literature isn't sure whether he and his family will be able to maintain their unusual vineyard in the long run, let alone expand it according to plan – although M'hudi is unique in a region in which hundreds of wine vineyards, some of them world famous, crowd each other out. M'hudi is the first wholly black-owned vineyard in South Africa. For this reason, Rangaka says, in 2009 he was invited to the White House to toast the first black president of the United States with his wine.

Even though the racist apartheid system has long been dismantled, whites still dominate South Africa's enological industry. Rangaka and his family bought the neglected wine farm in 2003 and named it M'hudi, after the heroine of an African novel, though it also means "harvester" in Setswana.

Though Rangaka, a landowner with a strong sense of purpose, praises the willingness of his neighbors from the Villiera and Koelenhof wine farms to assist and support him, M'hudi's business has struggled nonetheless. Wine sales have suffered, and wine tastings and the farm's hostelry had to be abandoned as they were unprofitable: "The wine drinkers here are white, and some of them mistrust 'black' wine, while the new black middle class is still learning to drink wine."

M'hudi produces a million liters of wine each year, including Chenin Blanc, Sauvignon Blanc, Chardonnay, Merlot, Shiraz, and Pinotage. Much of it is exported, especially to Great Britain and the United States.

If you want to visit the Rangakas' wine farm, you'll need to make an appointment. Someday, the wine tavern will, hopefully, be open every day again.

Address M'hudi Farm, Old Paarl Road Koelenhof, Stellenbosch 7605, Tel. +27/219886960, www.mhudi.com | **Getting there** By car: take N 1 in the direction of Somerset West, exit 32, M 15 in the direction of Koopmanskloof; after just over half a mile, turn left on R 101, Old Paarl Road | **Hours** By appointment only | **Tip** You can buy homemade juices, sauces, and other agricultural products at the BlueJay in Timberlea Fruit Farm on R 44 at the Helshoogte Road intersection.

56_ The Motor Museum
Old-timers in the midst of the Winelands

Looking at these four well-kept buildings among the picturesque surroundings of L'Ormarins wine farm from the outside, you'd think you were standing in front of some typical colonial vineyard storehouses. But in fact these structures shelter rarities of automotive history, which you wouldn't necessarily anticipate finding at the southern tip of Africa. More than 220 cars, motorcycles, and bicycles from all over the world, including names like Alfa Romeo, Ferrari, Bugatti, and Austrian Daimler Bergmeister, are neatly exhibited here. There is no comparable museum in all of Africa.

The Franschoek Motor Museum lays claims to showing the development of the automobile over the last century. That might be a bit exaggerated, despite this impressive armada of Daimler, Aston Martin, and Jaguar sports cars. The oldest piece on exhibit is a Beeston motor tricycle built in 1898. There are lots of racing cars, particularly Ferraris, but you can also marvel at the rare March 78B or a Chevron B25/3.

Since 1969, this wine farm has belonged to South-African billionaire and automobile aficionado Johann Rupert, who created the museum. His family and the museum made South Africa's headlines in 2008, when his son Anton had an accident on a country road in a Ferrari F50 that was to be exhibited at the museum. Johann Rupert finally published an open letter emphasizing that his son had by no means caused the accident by speeding, let alone through inattentiveness. Driving the museum's cars regularly is necessary, he explained, to keep them in good shape.

In his letter, the entrepreneur admitted that in his youth, he had done much worse things in his Alfa Romeo Gulia Super – it was probably in his family's genes, he joked.

Address Franschhoek Motor Museum/L'Ormarins wine farm, Franschhoek 7690 | **Getting there** By car: take N 2 to exit 47, turn right onto R 44, Adam Tass Street, turn left onto R 45; the wine farm will be on the right-hand side after about 9 miles | **Hours** Mon–Fri 10am–5pm, Sat and Sun 10am–4pm | **Tip** You can also visit the Huguenot Monument and the adjacent Huguenot Memorial Museum in Franschhoek on Lambrecht Street.

57 __ The Motorcycle Joint
Drive right up to the counter

The name of this beloved local haunt in Woodstock is NOB, which stands for "No Ordinary Burgers." Served on toasted rolls, the six-inch meat patties prepared right behind the counter of the bar are indeed impressive. Even a veggie burger made of mushrooms looks pretty macho. The burgers are available in numerous variations – but there isn't anything else on the menu. So if you're in the mood for a dainty salad, this isn't the place for you!

In fact, NOB is far more than just a great burger joint. The café is spectacular primarily because motorcycle bikers can drive their ponderous vehicles through the flattened entrance all the way up to the counter. Frequently, therefore, dozens of bikers in leather and rivets gather together here for a meal. Overall, the clientele is usually a colorful mixture of oddballs. Tourists are welcomed hospitably, though seldom find their way into this quiet street; located across a courtyard, it's not exactly easy to locate.

The walls of the funky eatery are decorated with garish Harley Davidson memorabilia, whiskey ads, and comic-book-style murals. The often blaring, old-fashioned jukebox and pinball machines from the 1960s add to the boisterous and irreverent atmosphere.

NOB is operated by Zezia and John Fourie, a young couple who clearly take a great deal of pleasure in what they do. If they run out of burgers, the Fouries just close up for the day. But if an exciting rugby or soccer game is on, normal operating hours go right out the window.

In the spring of 2015, the NOB was temporarily closed. Its famous hamburgers were only served in a mobile home lacquered jet-black – at concerts, festivals, and sporting events. The joint in Woodstock is to reopen soon; the bikers on the Cape are already drooling.

Address NOB Burger Cafe, 68 Bromwell Street, Woodstock, Cape Town 7915, Tel. +27/827844620, www.facebook.com/TheNobSA | **Getting there** By car: take R 102 Newmarket Street onto Albert Road, turn left onto Railway Street, left again at Mill Street, and take the first right onto Bromwell Street. By public transit: Bus 102, Kent Street stop | **Hours** Tue–Fri 11am–2:30pm & 5–9pm, Sat 10am–3pm | **Tip** The museum of the South African Air Force (Saaf Museum), is located on Piet Grobler Road about a mile away (Ysterplaat, Tel +27/215086576).

58 Muizenberg Station
A detour on the way to Simon's Town

If you decide to take a trip to Simon's Town on Cape Metrorail's train network, you should definitely buy a first-class ticket at Cape Town's modern central station, from which all of the local and long-distance trains depart. The tickets are hardly more expensive than second class, but the seats are better – if still rather Spartan. Above all, first class isn't as crowded. Furthermore, you should look for a car in which the windows open sideways so you'll have a good view of the coastline starting at the Zandvlei Lakes. Through the windows that can only be pulled halfway down, you'll have to stand to see out, because most of them are made of hard plastic and are filthy, blocked by signs or spray paint.

The stretch of tracks from Cape Town to Wynberg was opened as early as 1864 and was finally extended as far as Simon's Town. After passing through numerous unattractive suburban stops, it's worthwhile to take a break in Muizenberg, situated along the shores of False Bay. The late-Victorian-style station, with its beautiful red brick facade and conspicuous clock tower, was constructed in 1912, and replaced the original terminal building from 1881.

During the apartheid regime, the entrances to the station were strictly segregated by signs for whites and non-whites, as were the individual cars in the trains. At the end of the 19th century, Muizenberg – founded in 1743 by Dutch officer Wynard Muijs as a military post and then snatched from the Dutch by the British in the Battle of Muizenberg in 1795 – grew into a beach town and vacation destination, to which its Victorian architecture still bears testimony today.

Not far from the station, on the long sandy beach, is an excellent and well-known refuge for surfers with numerous surfing schools that welcome travelers.

Address 177 Main Road, Muizenberg, Cape Town 7950 | **Getting there** By car: From Cape Town, via M 3/M 4. By train: Metrorail Red Line, Muizenberg station | **Tip** The Muizenberg–St. James Walk, an approximately 20-minute stroll between the railroad tracks and the ocean from Muizenberg to St. James, is lovely.

59 The Mutual Building
Africa's first highrise

The facade itself is extraordinary: heads of baboons, elephants, and lions carved in granite look down on passersby. They are elements of the sculpted scenes and pictures of South Africa's colonial history that decorate the exterior of Cape Town's oldest high-rise, a tall-windowed affair that is mainly Art Deco in style, but also influenced by neoclassicism. The stone frieze, one of the longest in the world, displays portraits of men from such African ethnic groups as Xhosa, Kikuyu, and Zulu, as well as plants and animals characteristic of the region

Designed by South-African architect Fred Glennie, the Mutual Building – the original headquarters of the insurance firm Old Mutual – was a sensation upon its completion in 1939: with a height of 300 feet and 18 floors, and modeled after the Empire State Building in New York, it was the second-tallest building on the continent, after the Egyptian pyramids. It also featured Africa's fastest elevator.

The Mutual Building contains many architectural treasures – which becomes clear as soon as you set foot inside the imposing, 50-foot high, marble-lined entrance hall, with its steep staircase and gold-leaf ceiling. For a more intimate look, you will need an appointment, as the management permits only occasional viewings of the historic building, now converted to exclusive residential apartments. The most famous rooms in the "Mutual" are largely unused today. One of them is the Banking Hall, previously the insurance company's spacious cashiers' room, which, with its black marble, conveys a cool and austere feeling. Another is the assembly hall called the Fresco Room, with murals by the famous South-African artist Le Roux Smith Le Roux. His colorful paintings depict scenes from the country's history.

Address 14 Darling Street, City, Cape Town 8001, www.mutualheights.net | **Getting there** By public transit: Bus 106/107, Groote Kerk and Darling Street stop; "Hop on-Hop off" bus, Long Street Tour Office stop | **Hours** Not open to the public; viewings by appointment only | **Tip** The Old Post Office across the street is also in the Art Deco style. The biggest Art Deco ensemble of buildings is on Green Market Square: the Hotel Park Inn, the Protea Assurance Building, and Market House 3.

60 Mzoli's
Braii at the butcher of Gugulethu

The rustic restaurant, Mzoli's, in Gugulethu township on the fringes of Cape Town, lures a diverse mixture of customers. With its big tent-covered terrace, it is considered an inside tip for locals and for tourists who are particularly attracted to the low prices of the grilled entrees – but also for affluent Capetonians, who simply enjoy the down-to-earth meaty feasts and the folk festival atmosphere on summer days.

Celebrities and politicians are frequently among the clientele. At Mzoli's, South Africa's rainbow society seems to come to life.

In 2003, South African Mzoli Ngcawuzele had the brilliant idea of opening a butcher shop with a barbecue to attract as many people as possible. He started out with a kind of garage meat counter, which quickly grew into a real shop and restaurant with hundreds of seats. Guests first select what cuts they want from the shop's opulent display of meats and then tote their purchase on into the next room, to the professional grill masters. There are a number of spices and rubs to choose from, as well.

A DJ often heats up the atmosphere even further, and diners sing along and dance to the music. If you're lucky, you might even catch one of South Africa's most popular DJs, Christos, setting the place on fire.

You can buy accompaniments like salads, french fries, beer, and wine in the surrounding stores or bring your own. The most popular dishes at the South African *braai* parties are the *boerewors* – fatty sausages made of various kinds of meat, spicy lamb chops, and chicken thighs. You can use a knife and fork if you choose, or eat everything Mzoli style, with your hands.

Address Mzoli's Place, NY 115, Gugulethu, Cape Town 7751, Tel +27/216381355 |
Getting there By car: take N 2 in the direction of Muizenburg, exit Modderdam Road onto Robert Sobukwe Road, turn right on Modderdam Road, then Duinefontein Road, turn left on Klipfontein Road; after the railway crossing, take the first left |
Hours Daily 11am to late in the evening | **Tip** The Evangelical/Protestant project center, iThemba Labantu, in Philippi Township, is worth a visit (reservations required; New Eisleben Road, Tel +27/213712814, www.ithemba-labantu.co.za).

61 The National Library
Chilling out in the historic reading room

After marveling at the imposing columned portal of the splendid, completely white National Library at the entrance to Company's Garden, don't be afraid to go in.

First, you'll be greeted by some friendly people who'll ask to see your ID; then you'll pass through a security barrier, and suddenly you'll find yourself smack in the middle of South African intellectual life. Here, you can sit back and take a break from sightseeing for a bit, browse the reference library, or retreat into a corner of the reading room to peruse the national and international press. The venerable reading rooms with their old galleries supported by columns and stuffed with treasure troves of old books are enchanting. Dozens of students and scholars come here to study in complete quietude.

The National Library, which also has a branch in Pretoria, has everything that was and is printed in and about South Africa – books, maps, manuscripts, and all kinds of publications. There are also numerous unpublished papers, photos, and special collections. The most historically valuable pieces are restored and archived here.

Within this institution, which is closely connected with the country's universities and their 80 libraries, beats the heart of South Africa and its culture. Yet one deeply detrimental effect of apartheid is that still today, hardly more than half of the black South African population is able to read and write.

Until the end of the 20th century, South Africa had two great national libraries: the South African Library (founded in 1818 by Charles Somerset, the first civilian governor of the Cape colony), and the Pretoria State Library (founded in 1887). Both libraries merged with the National Library of South Africa in 1998, with its main branch in Cape Town.

Address National Library of South Africa, 5 Queen Victoria Street, City, Cape Town 8000, Tel +27/214246320, www.nlsa.ac.za | **Getting there** By public transit: Bus 106/107, Groote Kerk stop; "Hop on-Hop off" bus, St. George's Cathedral stop | **Hours** Mon, Tue, Thu, & Fri 9am–5pm, Wed 10am–5pm | **Tip** At the end of Company's Garden at Queen Victoria Street 62, there is an outreach of the National Library called the Centre for the Book in a spectacular Edwardian building.

62 — Nobel Square
South Africa's four Nobel Peace Prize winners

There they stand, in bronze and larger than life, next to one another on a pedestal made of granite in the middle of the Waterfront between the historic pump house and the V&A Hotel, on a small plaza that was renamed Nobel Square at the end of 2005. Although very different from one another, these four personalities have one thing in common: they all made history as South Africa's Nobel Peace Prize winners.

Albert Luthuli (1898–1967), chief of the Zulu tribe and former president of the African National Congress (ANC), was awarded the prize in 1960 for his nonviolent resistance against racial discrimination. He was the first African Nobel Peace Prize winner. Archbishop Desmond Tutu (b. 1931) received the distinction in 1984 as a committed opponent of apartheid and a symbolic figure of national unity. The 1993 Nobel Peace Prize went to Frederik Willem de Klerk (b. 1936), president of South Africa at the time, and Nelson Mandela (1918–2013), who was released from 27 years of imprisonment in 1990 and became South Africa's first black president, in 1994. They were both honored for the peaceful transition from the apartheid regime to a democratic constitution. Each statue at Nobel Square is decorated by a key quotation from the prize-winners set into the ground.

The fifth sculpture on the plaza, called *Peace and Democracy*, commemorates the contribution of women and children to the struggle against apartheid and for democracy.

The plaza and its works of art were the result of a nationwide competition, which was the idea of Ebrahim Rasool, then prime minister of the Western Cape. The competition winners were Cape Town artist Claudette Schreuders, for the four Nobel Peace Prize recipients; and 76-year-old Noria Mabassa, for *Peace and Democracy*.

Address Dock Road, V&A Waterfront, Cape Town 8001 | **Getting there** By public transit: Bus 104, Nobel Square stop; "Hop on-Hop off" bus, Aquarium stop | **Tip** Feel like stopping off for a beer in a pub? Try Ferrymans Tavern or Mitchell's Brewery on Dock Road at the Waterfront.

63__ The Noon Gun
Shooting off at midday since 1806

They're considered the oldest cannons still regularly firing in the world. Every day at high noon they announce the hour, and not just with a simple bang. The boom of the cannons being discharged daily (except Sundays) since 1806 – originally at the Waterfront and then from a plateau on Signal Hill high above the district of Bo-Kaap starting in 1902 – is so loud that the Capetonians set their watches by it, or start their break for lunch.

At about 11:30am, a marine appears at the shooting stand, initiating an eternal ritual. Next to the Lion Battery, he raises the finely folded flag of the South African Navy. Then he removes the two hoods – meant to protect the weapons from the occasionally raw weather on Signal Hill – from the original cannons coated with green patina, and opens a little white bag, from which 6.6 pounds of gunpowder are pressed into the cannons' muzzles. The soldier sets the detonator, which has been adjusted by the South African Astronomical Observatory since 1864, and asks the visitors to stand back at a safe distance from the cannons. Then he starts the countdown – first in larger intervals, then in seconds. Despite the fact that you know precisely when they'll fire, the inevitable clap of thunder enshrouded in a cloud of gun smoke still manages to startle you to the bone.

The cannons originally belonged to the artillery of the Castle of Good Hope and were used by the English at the Battle of Muizenberg in 1795. They were removed from their positions at the harbor at the beginning of the 20th century to Signal Hill, where they were used as a time signal for the ships at anchor, which were thus able to readjust their chronometers before sailing. In the meantime, the Lion Battery's Noon Guns on the military area, harboring still more ancient guns and cannons, have been fired off more than 65,000 times.

Address Military Road, Bo-Kaap, Cape Town 7764, Tel +27/217871257 | **Getting there** By car: from Buitengracht Street into Bo-Kaap via Military Street; then follow the signs, or else to the end of Longmarket Street, and then on foot | **Hours** 11am–4pm, cannon shot at 12 noon | **Tip** At the foot of Lion's Head on Upper Albert Road, you can have a look at the Cape Town International German School, founded in 1883.

64 The Oasis

Settling down in Company's Garden

Under gigantic ancient trees, surrounded by palms, exotic plants, and vines, under observation by squirrels and all kinds of birds, you'll sit in the shadowy oasis of Public Gardens Restaurant in total peace and quietude, far from the noise and the searing heat of nearby downtown. Right behind the white gate, with its freely hanging fire bell dating from 1855 and the bird pavilion, stands the little restaurant with numerous tables distributed in the garden.

Company's Garden, originally conceived by Jan van Riebeeck in 1652 on commission by the Dutch East India Company as a fruit and vegetable garden to feed the crews of ships, is now Cape Town's loveliest and oldest downtown park – a botanical garden surrounded by imposing historical buildings. Comprising nearly 20 acres, Company's Garden is comparatively small, but endowed with fascinating intensity. You can contemplate several monuments surrounding a statue of former Cape premier and diamond tycoon Cecil Rhodes, erected in 1909. It was Rhodes, by the way, who had the squirrels settled in the park, where they still frolic on the lawns. To boot, there are fountains, rose gardens, and omnipresent benches inviting you to linger awhile. And Table Mountain is always there in the backdrop. The grounds are a favorite location of international photographers and filmmakers.

Around the park, you will run into some of the city's architectural gems: the mighty Parliament building, constructed in the Victorian style and opened in 1885, for instance, and, right next to it, the Tuynhuys, the residence of the president when visiting Cape Town.

At the end of Company's Garden stands the National Gallery and the South African Museum.

Address Public Gardens, 19 Queen Victoria Street, City, Cape Town 8001, Tel +27/214232919 | **Getting there** at the end of Adderley Street, go on to Government Avenue. By public transit: Bus 101/106/107, Upper Long Street stop; "Hop on-Hop off" bus, St. George's Cathedral stop | **Hours** Dec–Feb, daily 7:30am–8:30pm; Mar–Nov, daily 7am–7pm | **Tip** There is a visitors' center on the west side of Company's Garden, and a public WLAN hotspot was installed in the middle of the park.

65 The Observatory
Reaching for the stars under Cape Town's skies

The popular district called Observatory owes its name to the Royal Observatory, a domed white building with ancient Greek architecture. Commissioned by Britain's King George IV in 1820, for a long time it was one of the world's most important observatories. For visitors wishing to view the sky through the McClean telescope and attend lectures, it's open regularly but relatively rarely: every second and fourth Saturday evening of the month.

Astronomical instruments and documents from two centuries can be admired here on floors that are moved in part by hydraulics. They were made at a time when astronomers were achieving epic scientific breakthroughs. Here, for instance, the exact distance between the Earth and the moon was measured for the first time. The city's terrific growth spelled a mounting problem for the observatory, however. Starting in the middle of the 20th century, Cape Town's increasingly bright sea of lights hampered the observation of the stars, and the venerable institution had to be abandoned as a place for research.

Today, the South African Astronomical Observatory (SAAO) resides 330 feet away in a pearl-white building that looks like a miniature White House. SAAO's most important telescope, the MeerKAT, is meanwhile in the semi-desert of Karoo, a plateau at an altitude of 5775 feet. South Africa is on the precipice of becoming one of the world's most important astronomical locations, and is playing a central role in the international telescope project Square Kilometre Array (SKA). SKA will be able to search the skies with 50 times more sensitivity and 10,000 times faster than all previous telescopes, making it possible to gaze into distant areas of the universe that have hardly been visible before. It won't be completely functional until 2024, however.

Address SAAO, Observatory Road, Observatory, Cape Town 7925, www.saao.ac.za | **Getting there** By car: take N3 (Nelson Mandela Boulevard), stay on the left to N2, Liesbeek Parkway exit towards the left, and take first right onto Observatory Road. By public transit: Golden Arrow bus, Observatory stop; Metrorail red line, Observatory station | **Hours** 2nd and 4th Sat each month, 8pm (www.saao.ac.za/about/visting/cape-town) | **Tip** The Tagore Late-Night Pub at 42 Trill Road is a gem among Observatory's copious array of bars. Live jazz is performed here every Friday (Tel +27/825634272).

66__The Old Biscuit Mill
Woodstock's "insider" Saturday market

Although the Neighbourgoods Market in the old industrial district of Woodstock is a regular item in the weekly schedule of many Capetonians, it hasn't lost any of its fascination. The market was brought to life in 2006 thanks to the initiative of two young Cape Town businessmen, and was an immediate hit.

Every Saturday, over 100 merchants and exhibitors, including local vintners, ecological farmers, flower vendors, bakers, craftspeople, and art dealers present their specialties. The market takes place in a converted old brick hall and in the courtyard of the Old Biscuit Mill. From cold-pressed juices to wood-fired pizza, the emphasis is on fresh merchandise and local products.

But one also comes to Neighbourgoods Market – which incidentally has a counterpart in Johannesburg – to see and be seen. Here, a mainly younger crowd meets up to eat, drink, and go shopping.

The Old Biscuit Mill, built at the end of the 19th century with a gigantic storage house and a square brick chimney, now has lots of fashionable restaurants, unusual designer stores, art and photography studios, and clothing and antique shops, plus live music events.

Many warehouses and factories are still vacant in this former industrial district along the railroad tracks. But the composition of the quarter is changing completely. In recent years, for instance, the buildings of the nearby Old Castle Brewery, a South African brewing company, were converted into a bustling creative center, populated by architectural offices, advertising agencies, and designer studios.

After dark, by contrast, Woodstock gets emptier and thus more dangerous.

Address Old Biscuit Mill, 373 Albert Road, on the corner of Mill Street, Woodstock, Cape Town 7915, Tel +27/214478194, www.theoldbiscuitmill.co.za | **Getting there** By car: take Strand Street onto R 102 (Newmarket Street) and onto Albert Road. By public transit: Bus 102 to Woodstock, Kent Street stop | **Hours** Neighbourgoods Market: Sat 9am–2pm; various operating hours for the other shops, cafes, and restaurants | **Tip** Albert Road, with its many designer shops, merits further investigation. You should certainly drop into the Delos Gallery (www.delos.co.za).

67 — The Operating Room
Where Professor Barnard transplanted his first heart

On December 3, 1967, the world held its breath: a heart was transplanted for the first time in medical history. A young surgeon at Groote Schuur Hospital in Cape Town had dared to perform this operation – and succeeded. It was an historic milestone in medicine that was later lauded with the same reverence as the landing on the moon. On a two-hour-long guided tour through the Heart of Cape Town Museum, which includes some of the original rooms of the legendary hospital, this decisive event will pass before your eyes through photos, films, and perfectly modeled wax figures in the heart surgeon's study. In the operating room, the dramatic hours between the fatal accident of 24-year-old heart donor Denise Darvall and the awakening of new heart owner Louis Washkansky are reconstructed.

It was the South-African physician Christiaan Barnard (1922–2001) who carried out this five-hour-long operation together with his 30-member team. Barnard had prepared for this moment for months. His transplant patient, Washkansky, survived the operation for 18 days before succumbing to pneumonia. Further spectacular heart transplants under the direction of Christiaan Bernard were to follow, making Groote Schuur Hospital a mecca for heart surgery. The hospital, situated below Devil's Peak since 1938 and named after a 17th-century Dutch farm (*groote schuur* means "big barn"), became the academic hospital of the nearby university's medical school, and a world-famous clinic.

Having turned into a media star overnight, Barnard, who then took up a jet-set lifestyle followed as zealously by the press as by medical periodicals, became a legend, and after Nelson Mandela the second-most popular South African of all time.

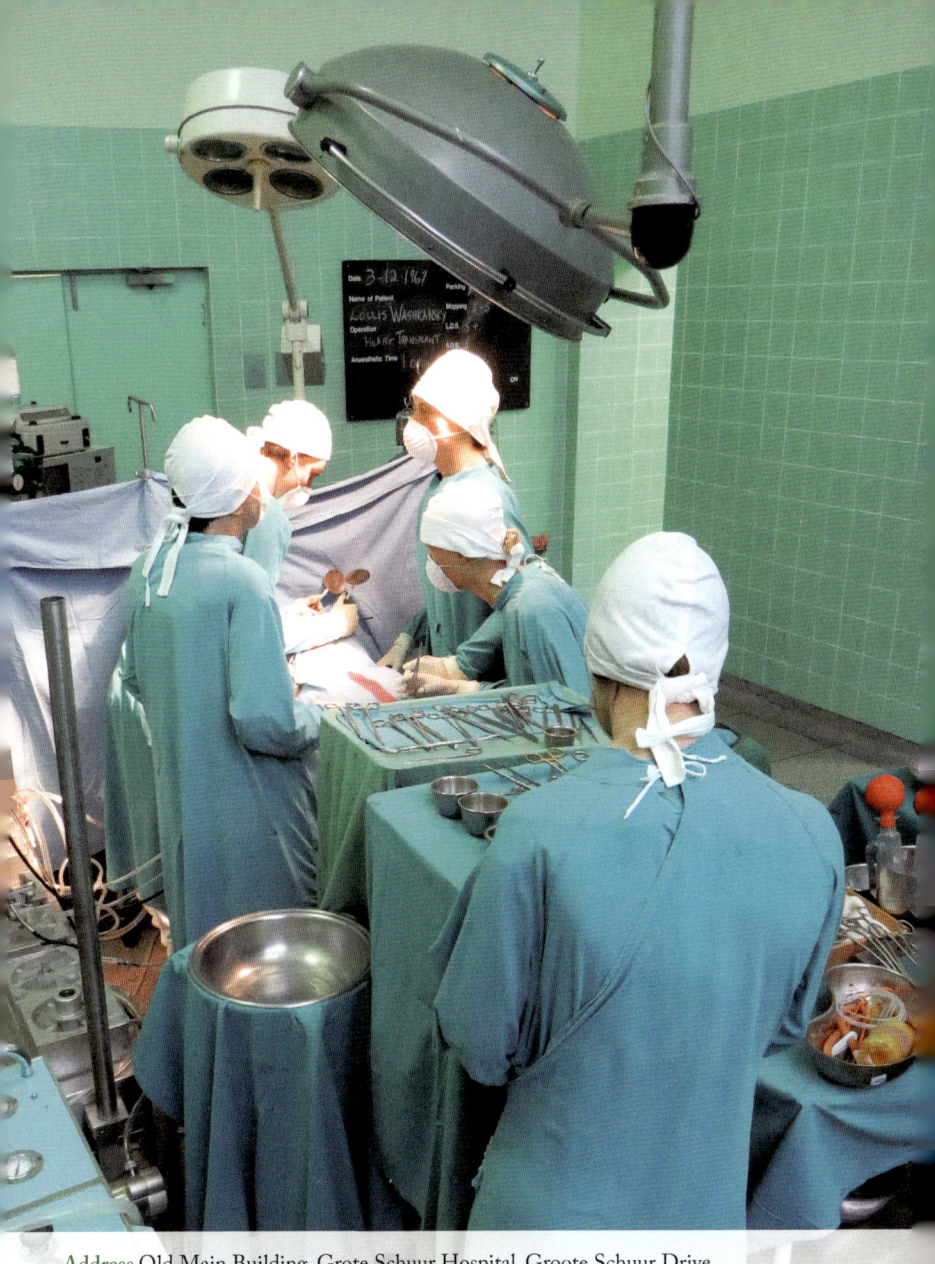

Address Old Main Building, Grote Schuur Hospital, Groote Schuur Drive, Observatory, Cape Town 7925, Tel +27/214041967, www.heartofcapetown.co.za | **Getting there** By car: take M 4 to the intersection with Station Road, which becomes Grotte Schuur Drive. By public transit: Metrorail, Observatory station; on foot from there via Station Road | **Hours** Daily 9am–5pm, guided tours at 9am, 11am, 1pm, 3pm, and at 5pm with a reservation only | **Tip** The old main portal of the hospital is worth seeing, as is the nearby University of Cape Town.

68 The Organ

Listening to the old masters in Groote Kerk

This organ, built in Holland, is really something. With nearly 6,000 pipes, it's considered the biggest in South Africa – and qualitatively one of the best. It wasn't installed in Groote Kerk (Afrikaans for "Great Church") until 1957 and was elaborately restored again in 2000. Connoisseurs revere its sound not only during services, but also at the numerous concerts taking place regularly in Groote Kerk, the so-called Mother Church of Calvinism, the Dutch Reformed faith.

Groote Kerk is right on Church Square – the plaza where the slaves from nearby Slave Lodge were auctioned off, sometimes in public, until 1834. The Reformed faith of the settlers came to the Cape with Jan van Riebeeck's arrival at Table Bay in 1652, and a much smaller church, the very oldest in South Africa, was built on this spot from 1678 to 1704, immediately next to the Dutch East India Company.

As the city expanded at terrific speed, the population outgrew the little church and it was torn down. In its stead, the current Groote Kerk was constructed between 1836 and 1941. Only the church tower remained unchanged – squeezed in and overshadowed today by a gigantic residential and commercial building.

The German sculptor Anton Anreith (1754–1822), who arrived in Cape Town in 1777 and was appointed master sculptor of the East India Company, created the pulpit, with its lions made out of Indian woods, in 1789. Still on view today, it is considered a masterpiece. It stands on exactly the same spot as the preceding church. One of Groote Kerk's attractions – the crypt in which nine governors of the Cape have found eternal rest – has been inaccessible since the heavy ceiling construction collapsed in 2012.

Address Groote Kerk, 43 Adderley Street, City, Cape Town 8001, Tel +27/214220569 | **Getting there** By public transit: Bus 106/107, Groote Kerk stop; "Hop on-Hop off" bus, St. George's Cathedral stop | **Hours** Mon–Fri 10am–2pm | **Tip** Visiting Slave Lodge at Church Square is a must. Now a museum, it used to hold up to 500 people, and impressively documents the history of slavery and apartheid. The Slavery Memorial, built in 2008, marks the injustice of slavery in South Africa.

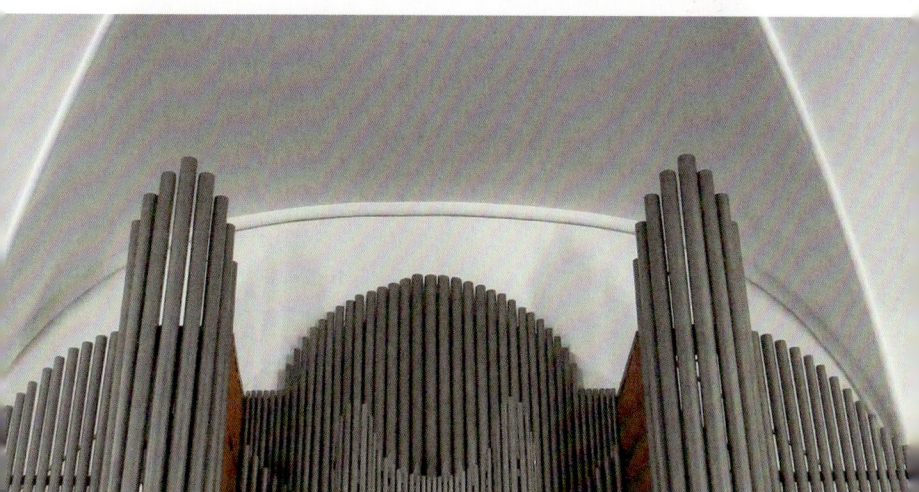

69 — The Ostrich Farm

Meet gigantic birds in the national park

Basically, the whole Cape peninsula is one sprawling national park. Breathtaking mountain massifs, exotic wildlife, endlessly long beaches, unique flora and fauna – and driving along the edge of Table Mountain National Park, just a short distance from the entrance to the Cape, you'll run into a group of animals commonly associated with South Africa, but which you wouldn't expect to find so close to the peninsula's southernmost tip. On enormous green meadows right in front of the mountains, innumerable ostriches are striding around, actually forcing you to stop for a while.

In 1996, two Germans got the idea to buy an old, run-down, inactive farm – nothing but ruins sticking out of the underbrush – and bring it back to life by founding a breeding ranch for ostriches. They now operate the fascinating Cape Point Ostrich Farm on 160 acres with more than 40 pairs of ostriches regularly producing offspring.

All in all, some 800 birds are living in the spacious compound, and as ostriches actually live for more than 70 years, you will find them in all age groups here. They grow and gain weight faster than any other animal, and they can run at speeds of up to 50 miles an hour.

This family operation, with its white, well-kept houses and stalls in typical Cape Dutch style, is a professionally managed business that includes a restaurant, which of course has all variations of ostrich meat on its menu. Cape Town's best eateries also purchase their ostrich meat from this farm.

You can buy all kinds of ostrich articles in the farm's shop, as well: tremendous, artistically decorated eggs, and a wide range of pocketbooks, shoes, and accessories – all made of ostrich leather.

Address Cape Point Ostrich Farm, P.O. Box 867, Sun Valley, Cape Town 7985, Tel +27/217809294, www.capepointostrichfarm.com | **Getting there** By car: take M 65; the farm is located about a quarter mile north of the entrance to Table Mountain National Park | **Hours** Daily 9:30am–5:30pm, guided tours: you can find out everything about these unusual flightless birds, and if you're lucky, you can watch chicks hatching | **Tip** Coming from Kommetjie, and shortly before turning left in Scarborough in the direction of Cape Point, you'll reach Camel Rock, named for its humplike shape.

70   Oude Bank Bakkerij
Considered the best bakery on the Cape

De Oude Bank Bakkerij is a part of Schoon de Companje ("Schoon Company"). Young master baker Fritz Schoon made this bakery the core of an ambitious family project. A colorful marketplace and an unusual bistro occupy two floors of this corner house, which was formerly a bank. It's a favorite among students and employees of the nearby University of Stellenbosch. The elaborately restored rooms lined with pinewood resemble a small and lively market. You can even see into the bake house, where many bread specialties are produced in the big woodstove.

All around Oude Bakkerij there are fruit and vegetable stands, as well as a "Butchers' Boutique," a coffee roastery, a restaurant, an ice-cream parlor, a bar, a wine tavern, and a number of kitchens. Schoon emphasizes that nearly all of the products are organic and locally produced. Many items are in fact created on the spot, such as bread, ice cream, sauces, and sausages. The young entrepreneur brought his whole family together to make his dream come true: his wife manages the butcher shop and his sister oversees the ice-cream parlor, while his mother is the interior decorator.

The restaurant sometimes looks like the living room of a commune, with rustic wooden tables, a long dining table, and a cozy sofa corner. Nothing in the establishment is inimical to pleasure: in addition to vegetarian delicacies, there are also richly topped pizzas, and juicy and hefty hamburgers to go with the local wines and beers. You can test the house's breads with freshly prepared meze, pies, and vegetable creams, or various cheeses and meats. Cola and other commercial soft drinks are replaced on the menu by fresh juices and a slew of mixed tea or coffee beverages. Fritz Schoon loves to host live music here.

Address 7 Church Street, Stellenbosch 7600, Tel +27/218832187 | **Getting there** By car: take N2 and R310 to Stellenbosch, follow in the direction of Dorp Street, then left on Piet Retief Street; then take the first street to the right into Church Street | **Hours** Tue–Fri 7am–6pm, Sat 8am–6pm, Sun 8am–1pm, dinner and live music Wed & Sat 6–10pm | **Tip** Church Street is full of interesting galleries featuring South-African artists. The Dorp Straat Gallery, for instance, is right next to Oude Bakkerij.

71_Panama Jacks
Offbeat fish restaurant hidden in the harbor

Panama Jacks calls itself "Cape Town's best-kept secret" – no wonder, what with its hard-to-find location deep inside the harbor. The best way to get there is to ask. You have to pass through two harbor controls, stopping in front of a barrier upon entering and exiting, where you must open the trunk of your car for inspection.

Once you've passed the ships, containers, gigantic warehouses, supersized derricks, and gigantic drilling rigs, you'll find a place that looks from the outside like a lengthy barracks bedecked with a blue-and-white awning. But inside the spacious restaurant, a somewhat dark ambience with an unusually inviting atmosphere awaits you. Everything looks a bit antiquated and improvised, but the extremely fresh seafood fulfills the justifiably high expectations of a harborside restaurant. Many Capetonians enjoy having lunch here, while the seamen and sailors drink beer from the barrel at the long counter during their noonday break.

Founded back in 1989 as a service and catering station to the Royal Yacht Club, Panama Jacks quickly got a license as a public restaurant. Staples on the menu include fresh lobster in many variations, priced according to weight and selected by the customer from a saltwater tank; abalone (ear shell); yellowtail; cod; and sushi of all kinds. There are always so-called linefish fresh from the hook, otherwise known as "the catch of the day." More than 120 wines are available to accompany your meal.

In the summertime, reservations are strongly recommended; out of season, you can try your luck. The manager will generally always find you a seat, and seldom sends anyone away hungry who has managed to find their way through the industrial harbor to the restaurant's door.

Address Panama Jacks, Quay 500 Cape Town Docks, Foreshore, Cape Town 8001, Tel +27/214473992 or +27/214481080, www.panamajacks.net | **Getting there** By car: take Eastern Mole Road, Quay 500, the third street behind the Royal Yacht Club in the freight harbor | **Hours** Sun–Fri noon–2:30pm & 6:30–10:30pm | **Tip** As long as you're here, take the opportunity to have a closer look around the industrial harbor.

72 Panorama Highway
Where you meet wild baboons

Driving from the Cape, the sight that awaits you when you leave M 65 and turn on M 4 toward Simon's Town is simply splendid: far below Panorama Highway lies the coastline, with breathtaking Smitswinkel Bay and a vista all the way to Cape Point. Tiny Smitswinkel Bay Village, with its handful of houses, is accessible only on foot or by boat. Farther down the road, past Danger Rock and Miller's Point, you often run into baboons.

As on the Cape, the diurnally active animals sit here peacefully by the roadside, looking almost bored. You can observe them from your car and, if you find a little parking bay, you can also get out. But please: keep your distance. Don't feed them by any means, let alone touch them. (Feeding them is punishable!) Baboons are erratic; they are omnivorous, and can quickly snatch a picnic basket or grab handbags through open car windows.

The male baboons are considerably bigger and heavier than the females. Their doglike snouts and the short space between their eyes are prominent. At night, they sleep in trees or withdraw to the rocky cliffs. They live on the southern Cape peninsula in the wild, as in the rest of southern and eastern Africa, and are classified as threatened by extinction.

There are several hundred baboons living on the Cape. A research project initiated by the Cape administration is specifically monitoring the chacma baboon species. The monkeys live in groups of up to forty animals, and there are about a dozen of these communities on the 32-mile-long and 10-mile-wide peninsula.

Near Table Mountain, you can repeatedly run into baboons, as well; there's even a small colony on the plateau.

Address M 4 between Smitswinkel Bay and Miller's Point, Cape Town 7975 | **Getting there** By car: take M 4 from Cape Town or the Cape | **Tip** The project "Baboon Matters," a baboon protection initiative in Kommetjie, offers guided tours and lectures upon reservation (Tel +27/217857493). Seaforth Beach nearby is a small and lovely bathing beach protected from the wind, shortly before Boulders Beach, known for its penguin colony.

73 Peers Cave
Traces of human life in the Stone Age

The caves discovered by Victor Peers in 1927 are still shrouded in mystery today. Here, high up on the mighty rock massif above Fish Hoek, the singing of Xhosa women occasionally resounds. Equipped with cult artifacts and candles, they hold services in the caves in order to connect with their ancestors – who were actually only 16th-century immigrants.

But thousands of years previously, human beings had already lived in Peers Cave. You can find primitive red rock drawings on the ceilings of this location declared a national cultural monument. Even today, amongst the pebbles, there are little corners and splinters of archaic Stone Age tools.

Peers – a hobby archaeologist – and his son Bertie found the site and discovered nine graves, including the remains of the "Fish Hoek Man." The age of this skeleton was first estimated at 15,000 years. Archaeologists, who still criticize Peers for his negligent dealings with the site, believe that the bones can hardly be older than 7,300 years.

If you want to visit Peers Cave you will need to bear some things in mind. Coming from county road M 64, there is an access with room to park from which the cave can be reached via a footpath about 1.25 miles in length. However, there are strict warnings against walking alone or as a couple through the dense overgrowth. Those living nearby also warn that no car should be left unguarded.

If you would like to go up to the caves from a more secure place, drive instead to the parking lot of the sports club in Fish Hoek. Then, however, it is about a 1.25-mile hike that is steep in parts; heavy shoes are indispensable. But the visit is worthwhile thanks to the panoramic view across the broad valley all the way to False Bay.

Address Silvermine Nature Reserve, Ou Kaapse Weg, Fish Hoek, Muizenberg, Cape Town 7966 | **Getting there** By car: take M3, then M4 in the direction of Muizenburg and Fish Hoek, turn right on M64; the parking lot is on the right-hand side after 1.25 miles; advisable only with experienced guides in small groups. Alternative: take Kommetje Road in Fish Hoek, turn right onto 20th Avenue; after about 300 feet, there are sports fields with relatively secure parking lots on the right-hand side | **Tip** The Fish Hoek Valley Museum, on Central Circle in Fish Hoek, offers further information about Peers Cave and the history of whaling (Tel +27/217821752, open Tue–Sat 9:30am–12:30pm).

74__ The Penguin Colony
Witness a miracle of nature in Boulders

What a surprise – penguins in Africa! You normally associate these impressively striding seabirds with Antarctica's icy landscapes. Portuguese seafarer Vasco da Gama, the first to discover the sea route to India via the Cape of Good Hope, was nonplussed when he ran into penguins, with their tuxedo-like plumage, at Mossel Bay in 1497. His log entry is the first known mention of the existence of black-footed penguins on the African coasts.

Today, these unusual seabirds are still living on the southwestern shoreline. But the black-footed penguin is a threatened species. A hundred years ago, there were millions of them in Africa; now, only somewhat more than 20,000 of them remain in Angola, Namibia, and South Africa. Nowhere, however, can you observe them better than at Boulders Beach in Simon's Town.

You don't necessarily need to go into the national park to see penguins. You can also find some of these seemingly stoical birds on the nearby beaches and dunes. But paying the price of admission to the state-run facility is worth it: on curving wooden walkways through the dunes to the beach, you can view the breeding grounds and the habitat of more than 1,000 penguins close up.

Boulders Beach belongs to Table Mountain National Park and is accordingly protected and cleaned. Animal caregivers also tend to the breeding grounds in the dunes, and you can observe breeding penguins in little Plexiglas kennels or in simple plastic containers dug into the ground. The seabirds – who sometimes sound like braying donkeys – have meanwhile grown so accustomed to humans that they wander around fearlessly, sometimes even entering the gardens of the neighboring houses. In Simon's Town, traffic signs warn you to watch out for errant penguins.

Address Boulders Penguin Colony, Boulders Beach, Simon's Town, Cape Town 7975, www.sanparks.co.za | **Getting there** By car: take M3 via Muizenburg to Simon's Town, then follow Queens Road to the Penguin Colony, then turn left. By public transit: Metrorail red line, Simon's Town station (last stop) | **Hours** Dec–Jan, 7am–7:30pm; Feb–Mar, 8am–6:30pm; Apr–Sep, 8am–5pm; Oct–Nov, 8am–6:30pm | **Tip** You can swim among the penguins at the usually empty beach diagonally across from the protected facility, one exit farther down Queens Road after the Boulders colony.

75 — The Plateau
Having a good time on Table Mountain

The gondola ride up the steep slope of Table Mountain lasts about six minutes. If you squeeze yourself into the cabin with a capacity of 64 passengers and try to get a good position at the window, you'll discover that the gondola, hovering just a short distance above the rugged cliffs, rotates a complete 360 degrees during its ascent to the plateau – which means that wherever you stand, everybody sees the steadily shrinking City Bowl, the harbor, Lion's Head, and Signal Hill, equally well. The cable car, with its 2300-foot ascent, has been running since 1929, and has been equipped with the special revolving Swiss gondolas since 1998.

You should set aside a good amount of time for your exploration of Table Mountain because it offers a complex adventure. There are unbelievable panoramic views of the city, of the Cape Flats, the Twelve Apostles mountain range, and the beaches of Clifton and Camps Bay. But above all, the plateau will enchant you: it's a cosmos in itself. Resembling a garden planted on an enormous flat roof, the vegetation here is unique and diverse. In this high-altitude "Cape Floral Kingdom," more than 1,000 plants thrive, some of them on Table Mountain exclusively. There are rare breeds of fynbos here, as well as South Africa's national flower, the king protea.

There are various routes for climbing up Table Mountain from the bottom – more challenging from the north side; easier from the Botanical Garden in Kirstenbosch. But you can also simply start from high up on the plateau, where you'll find five excellently prepared hiking trails, three of which can be easily completed within 30 minutes. With each step away from the cable car station, you'll find your surroundings more tranquil and meditative.

Address Lower Cable Station, Tafelberg Road, Gardens, Cape Town 7941, Tel +27/21424818, www.tablemountain.net | **Getting there** By car: to Kloof-Nek traffic circle between Table Mountain and Lion's Head. By public transit: Bus 106/107, Kloof Nek stop, then about a mile on foot; bus 110, lower terminus; "Hop on-Hop off" bus, Table Mountain Cableway stop | **Hours** Summer, 8am–9:30pm (last descent); winter, 8:30am–6pm (last descent); closed in case of high winds | **Tip** Ride up the mountain only with good weather. You can take a picnic basket and a bottle of wine with you, but there's also a restaurant at the summit station.

76_Pollsmoor Prison
Lunch in Mandela's prison

The most infamous prison on the Cape is situated across from picturesque Steenberg Wine Farm, with its luxury hotel and spacious golf course.

After being greeted by the friendly officers and passing through the rather lax security procedures at the entrance gate, and strolling along the miles of streets on these vast grounds, you will intuit very little about the brutal reality of this institution. After all, this is Pollsmoor Maximum-Security Prison. A number of the complexes are surrounded twofold and threefold by barbed wire, and 13-foot-high walls block off every gaze. In the middle of this prison – feared for its brutal gang wars – with some 7,000 inmates and 1,300 guards, sits one of the strangest restaurants in South Africa.

Idlanathi (which translates as "eat with us") advertises itself with the fact that South Africa's national hero Nelson Mandela spent six years of his 27-year imprisonment in Pollsmoor. However, the restaurant, with the sober ambience of a particularly clean, simple canteen, could also boast of its excellent food for economical prices. Fried eggs with bacon or a steak sandwich cost about two euros each; a hefty portion of roast octopus with salad, less than three euros; and a pile of delicious spareribs with french fries is the most expensive item on the menu, at 4.5 euros.

The service is particularly nice – after all, inmates have to earn the coveted jobs here, and the waitlist for those positions is long. The garish orange uniforms underneath the white smocks and shirts of the cooks and waiters – and the presence of uniformed guards – will remind you that this is not your typical eatery. Alcohol, of course, isn't served. Tips are also frowned on.

Address Idlanathi, Pollsmoor Prison, Steenberg Road, Tokai, Cape Town 7945, Tel +27/217001270 | **Getting there** By car: take N 2 (Nelson Mandela Boulevard), stay on the right-hand side to M 3 (Rhodes Drive), exit 21, turn right on Tokai Road, then left on M 42 (Steenberg Road) – the prison is on the left side after a quarter mile. By public transit: Golden Arrow bus, Pollsmoor Prison stop | **Hours** Mon–Sun 7am–2pm | **Tip** There are lovely jazz and other concerts in the park-like garden of Steenberg Wine Farm during the summer.

77 _ The Quarry
Forced labor on Robben Island

"They wanted to break our spirit, but we sang songs of freedom … They told us, 'No singing while working.' So we really felt the severity of the work." Nelson Mandela soberly described everyday life in Limestone Quarry during his 18 years in Robben Island prison. Today, the name is symbolic for the brutal persecution of the freedom fighters during apartheid. For 3,000 people, Robben Island meant isolation, the daily torment of hard labor with pickaxes, and the arbitrary brutality of the regime's guards. Mandela contracted a permanent eye ailment from the relentless exposure to the glaring sun. Standing in front of the deserted quarry (walking around in it is forbidden) on a hot summer day, you can have some intimation of the agonies of the prisoners.

If the rocks of Blue Quarry, Van Riebeecks Quarry, and Limestone Quarry could talk, they would tell a story of suffering going back to the 17th century. Here, convicts, slaves, and brutally exploited day laborers chopped rocks for harbors, houses, and streets on the coast. Limestone Quarry, which is a part of the Robben Island guided tour, was established by the Dutch colonial lords. They – and after them, the British colonial masters – used the island mainly as a penal colony, but it also served as a depository for lepers and "madmen."

Today, the island, with its quarries, penitentiary buildings, and Nelson Mandela's isolation cell (maintained in its original condition), is a national monument and a fascinating museum commemorating the agonizing path of the freedom fighters toward equality and democracy. If you go on the well-organized guided tour lasting four hours, you'll realize that there was no escape from this windswept island, with its view of nearby Table Mountain and the city.

Address Robben Island, Cape Town 7400 | **Getting there** Guided tours (the only way to visit the island) depart from Nelson Mandela Gateway, Waterfront, V&A Clock Tower, Cape Town 8001 | **Hours** Ferries depart at 9am, 11am, & 1pm, depending on the weather. Buy tickets early, as tours are often sold out days in advance, Tel +27/2141342201; Nelson Mandela Gateway: info@robben-island.org.za; tickets online: www.webtickets.co.za | **Tip** The ferry ride to Robben Island is also worth taking for its splendid panorama of Cape Town and Table Mountain.

78 — The Racetrack
Betting on horses at the city gates

The importance of horse racing and horse breeding in South Africa goes back to the historic phase of English rule. There are twelve racetracks with some 440 meetings a year in South Africa, and people bet like mad at the daily races. One of the most important is the J&B Met in the Kenilworth District of Cape Town.

But the J&B Met, sponsored by the whiskey brand of the same name, is much more than Cape Town's biggest horse race: together with the L'Ormarins Queen's Plate, which also takes place on Kenilworth Racecourse, it is the social event of the year on the Cape.

Every January, some 50,000 people make the pilgrimage to the little suburb between Wynberg and Claremont, transforming Kenilworth into the Mecca of South African racing, and the racetrack into a catwalk of vanities. Everybody who is somebody is there; Cape Town's influential firms and chic shops have their own tents and boxes. Champagne flows in streams and people exhibit themselves in the most outlandish outfits, competing for fashion prizes that are awarded on the big stage and dominate the press the next morning.

It was the British Cape governor Charles Somerset who steered South African horse breeding and racing into orderly channels at the beginning of the 19th century, turning them into flourishing businesses. Although Johannesburg also became a horse-racing center with the discovery of the first diamonds in 1871, and of gold later on, Cape Town has always maintained its position. At first, horse races on the Cape were held at Green Point, but they have been on the Kenilworth Racecourse since 1882. After a stormy history, the Metropolitan Mile, established in 1883, turned into the J&B Met in 1978.

Address Kenilworth Racecourse, Kenilworth, Cape Town 7709, Tel +27/217971343 | **Getting there** By car: take M4 (Main Road) or M5 to Kenilworth; entrances to the racetrack on Rosmead Avenue and Wetton Road. By public transit: Metrorail Cape Town to Simon's Town line, get off at Kenilworth station | **Hours** More than 20 races a year, mainly during the South African summer | **Tip** At St. James Church in Kenilworth, members of the military arm of the Pan Africanist Congress (PAC) committed a massacre during services on July 25, 1993. Eleven people were killed by grenades and rifle bullets and more than 50 were injured, some of them severely.

79   The Revolver
Memorial against violence

There are 30 replicas of this work of political art in places around the world – but here in Cape Town the iconic bronze gun with a knot in its muzzle has special meaning. This metropolis, with 4 million inhabitants, has often been South Africa's "murder capital." This statistics-based title is all the more shameful considering that in only a few corners of Latin America and in war zones are crime and violence worse than in South Africa. While there is little danger for tourists, the South Africans have been living for many years with the ugly reality of crime running riot and of everyday brutalities. The "Non-Violence" sculpture in the middle of the V&A Waterfront is a symbol for the peaceful solution of conflicts.

The Swedish artist, Carl Fredrik Reuterswärd, created the sculpture of a colossal and alienated Colt Python as a reaction to the shooting of the musician John Lennon – the ex-Beatle had been Reuterswärd's personal friend. The original sculpture stands at the United Nations Headquarters in New York City. The replica in Cape Town was unveiled in 1999.

This symbol is also the logo of the globally active "Non-Violence Project Foundation," supported by Yoko Ono, Ringo Starr, and Paul McCartney, among many others. In South Africa, the organization, based in Switzerland, is collaborating on projects to resolve conflicts in the townships, where the people are justifiably most afraid of violence. Guns, however, don't play as great a role in crime here as in the United States or in Mexico.

South Africa suffers not only from criminal violence, but also from domestic violence against women and children. Women's associations say that, statistically, one out of two South African women experiences violence during her lifetime.

Address Victoria & Alfred Waterfront, Breakwater Boulevard, Cape Town 8002, www.nonviolence.com | **Getting there** By public transit: Bus 104, Waterfront stop; "Hop on-Hop off" bus, Aquarium stop | **Tip** You can find unusual articles, such as Christmas decorations, made year-round in the Red Shed Craft Workshop, somewhat hidden at the edge of the nearby shopping center (open daily 9am–9pm).

80 The Rhodes Memorial
Resting at the political visionary's feet

The huge monument to Cecil Rhodes (1853–1902) is located close to the Botanical Gardens at a prominent position high above Cape Town. A long and narrow road behind the university below Devil's Peak leads up to this columned structure, erected out of Cape granite in 1912 by English architect Herbert Baker (1862–1946).

It's worth the drive for a little picnic, to take in the phenomenal panorama, and to get a bit closer to this eternally controversial figure of South African history – this imperialist of the British Crown, who believed that Africa would be under British rule, all the way from the Cape to Cairo. The bronze statue called *Physical Energy* by the British sculptor George Frederic Watts (1817–1904), depicting a rider "energetically" looking northward perched high above Cape Town, is supposed to symbolize this.

At the age of 17, Rhodes was sent by his family to his brother's cotton plantation in South Africa for health reasons. It was just at the time when the first diamonds were being found. The brothers went into the jewelry business and made a gigantic fortune in only a few years with their gold and diamond mines. Young Rhodes was a cofounder of De Beers Consolidated Diamond Mines and finally gained a monopoly over southern African diamond production, thus becoming one of the richest men in the world. He founded a colonial empire extending far beyond South Africa. Today's Zambia and Zimbabwe were already named Northern and Southern Rhodesia after him during his lifetime.

Rhodes became prime minister of the Cape colony in 1890. Caught up in the conflicts and the Second Boer War (1899–1902), he died in Muizenberg at the age of 49.

Address Rhodes Memorial, Rhodes Drive, Groote Schuur Estate, Cape Town 7764, www.rhodesmemorial.co.za | **Getting there** By car: take M3, exit 8 (Rondebosch), via Rhodes Drive up to the end of Rhodes Memorial Street (there are signs) | **Tip** Behind the memorial stands a restaurant with a tea garden that's open daily from 9am to 5pm. Also interesting is the Rhodes Cottage Museum in Muizenberg – the vacation cottage in False Bay in which Rhodes spent the last days of his life and, suffering from tuberculosis, died of a heart attack in 1902.

81 The Rugby Museum
Where the Springboks are revered

Opened in 2013, this museum can keep pace with the multimedia worlds of the great European football clubs in Munich, Barcelona, and Manchester. Maybe everything here is on a slightly smaller scale, but as far as the effects, didactic structuring, and the arc of suspense are concerned, the new Springbok Experience Rugby Museum is a thrill. Even if you aren't terribly interested in rugby, the museum will help you to grasp the national fascination with this South African institution, which unleashes great emotions.

The history of the Springboks will teach you a great deal about the history of rugby, which is also a definitive hunk of South African history. A South African team challenged Great Britain to an international game for the first time in 1891, in gold-green jerseys and white trousers. It was the beginning of an era of sports competitions with all of the world's rugby nations that lasted for decades.

But the anti-apartheid movement also escalated over rugby. Athletic isolation as well as boycotts and unrest when the Springboks played were the results. Then came the political revolution, and their return to the international stage. The Springboks of the new South Africa became world champions in rugby in 1995, and again in 2007.

Sixty audio-visual stations and many in-person presentations make discovering the story of the Springboks and rugby in South Africa an entertaining and interesting adventure. The museum offers a high-tech experience of rugby from a variety of perspectives. A multimedia cinema introduces visitors to all of the force and intensity of the sport, but also the refinement. Visitors meet the idols of past and present, and communicate with them via interactive touchscreens.

Address Springbok Experience Rugby Museum, Portswood House, V&A Waterfront, Cape Town 8002, Tel +27/214184741, www.sarugby.co.za | **Getting there** By public transit: Bus 104, Waterfront stop; "Hop on-Hop off" bus, Aquarium stop | **Hours** Daily, 10am–6pm | **Tip** Cape Town's rugby stadium, the Newland Stadium, on Boundary Road in Newlands, opened in 1890 with a capacity of 51,000 people.

82 Rust en Vreugd
18th-century Cape architecture

This building is so far from the many sights around the Company's Garden – the beloved public park – that few visitors happen to stray this way. One might almost think that the Capetonian museum directors welcome this unpopularity. The rather sober and poorly illuminated rooms in Rust en Vreugd harbor an important annex of Iziko – the umbrella organization of state-run South African museums – together with offices, meeting rooms, and a cafeteria. Too many visitors would seem like a disturbance. But the house is worth seeing because it's one of Cape Town's loveliest.

The building was constructed in 1778 – between the city and the farms at the base of Table Mountain at the time – and is considered the best-conserved specimen of late 18th-century Cape architecture. Willem Cornelis Boers, a high-ranking colonial officer of the Dutch East India Company had this estate designed and built by the young French architect Louis Thibault, who had recently immigrated to Cape Town. It will enchant you with its Baroque ornaments on the windows, doors, and balconies, created by Cape sculptor Anton Anreith.

Rust en Vreugd (which means "linger and enjoy") belonged to the Reformed Church for decades and was a teacher-training school; it later became Cape Town High School. The building's character remained unchanged down through the centuries – perhaps precisely because the house and the garden were situated far from the expanding boom town. In the 1990s, the estate was thoroughly renovated.

Besides Iziko ("hearth" in the Xhosa language), it now shelters the collection of watercolors donated to the people of South Africa in 1965 by the avid art collector and entrepreneur William Fehr.

Address Rust en Vreugd, 78 Buitenkant Street, Gardens, Cape Town 8000, Tel +27/214813903, www.iziko.org.za/museums/rust-en-vreugd | **Getting there** By public transit: Bus 103, Roeland Street stop; "Hop on-Hop off" bus, SA Jewish Museum stop | **Hours** Mon–Fri 10am–5pm | **Tip** You can see how affluent 18th-century Capetonians lived in the perfectly conserved and furnished Koopmans de Wet House on Strand Street. Bertram House, at the end of Government Avenue, is the only surviving Georgian-style town house in Cape Town, and is open to the public.

83__The Saltwater Pool
Relaxed swimming near the breakwater

It's no exaggeration to say that Sea Point Pavilion Swimming Pool, situated right on the 3-mile-long Sea Point Promenade bordering the Atlantic Ocean with its high waves, is one of the loveliest and most extraordinary open-air public pools in the world.

You wouldn't venture into the ocean here because of the tricky currents, rocky cliffs, and frigid water of the Benguela Current. In the pool, however, the proximity of the ocean provides an exhilarating atmosphere, particularly when a wave hits the walls and kicks up a chilly spray of water.

Built during apartheid, Sea Point was a strictly white middle-class district. Thoroughly renovated during the 2000s, the swimming complex sports a 164-foot Olympic-size pool, a children's pool, a "fun" pool, and a pool for divers with a diving board 16.4 feet high.

The pools' purified and filtered seawater is perfectly clear and constantly monitored. The complex is open year-round, and the water is unheated. During the winter, it is seldom warmer than 59 degrees Fahrenheit, but in the summer, its temperature is splendid.

With fewer visitors during the week, you can relax – with a view of the Atlantic and Robben Island in front of you and Table Mountain behind you – beneath shady palm trees (in contrast to many of Cape Town's beaches, where you'll usually search in vain for a place in the shade).

Sea Point's beach promenade, an extension of Green Point's promenade, is a favorite place for jogging and other athletic activities. A broad lawn right next to the water invites you to have a picnic – far from the traffic, and always with a cool breeze.

Address Sea Point Pavilion, Lower Beach Road, Sea Point, Cape Town 8005, Tel +27/214343341 | **Getting there** By public transit: Bus 104, Sea Point Pool stop; "Hop on-Hop off" bus, Sea Point stop | **Hours** Oct–Apr, daily 7am–7 pm, May–Sep, daily 8:30am–5pm | **Tip** With its good restaurant and lush garden, Winchester Mansion Hotel, built in 1922 in the Cape Dutch style, stands out from a mass of stereotypical homes from the 1960s and 1970s. There are jazz concerts in the courtyard on Sundays.

84 The San Centre
The bush people's old country

When the very friendly tour guide starts laughing and falls back into his native tongue, you'll know just how enormously foreign another language can be. No other commonly known dialect has a single similarity with the mixture of clicking and snapping sounds that characterize the San language, which is extremely difficult to imitate. At !Kha ttu – a splendid wildlife park with a cultural and educational center, simple guest houses, and a recommendable restaurant with African cuisine – everything is dedicated to information about the San.

The bush people can justly lay claim to having been the first inhabitants of the Cape region more than 20,000 years ago, until they were driven out by the warlike Hottentots – long before the region's painful history of displacement, conquest, and battles began. In the colonial times of the 18th and 19th centuries, the rather small bush people were often hunted and killed legally, like animals. At times, the San were threatened by extermination.

The !Kha ttu documentation center, with its vividly painted scenes, is dedicated to the history of the San, of whom only about 4,000 are left in South Africa. Tours lasting about three hours each through the hilly bush country with its zebras, antelopes, and gazelles, are available. An authentically built traditional San village with roundhouses visualizes the everyday life of these peaceful hunters and gatherers.

In such southern African countries as Botswana and Namibia, the San languish on the margins of society. In order to preserve this endangered culture, for several years now !Khwa ttu has been offering a training course to become a tour and nature guide to small groups of bush people from the neighboring countries.

Address !Khwa ttu Cultural Village, R 27 West Coast Road, Yzerfontein, Cape Town 7351, www.khwattu.org | Getting there By car: from Cape Town take the N 1 expressway, then county road R 27 north for about 43 miles. | Hours Daily 9am–5pm, guided tours at 10am & 2pm | Tip In West Coast National Park, 12.5 miles north of !Khwa ttu on R 27, you'll find an almost untouched natural reservation with a lagoon, beaches, and islands – the natural habitat of thousands of seabirds, many tortoises, antelopes, ostriches, and zebras (Tel +27/227722144).

85 __ The Seven Memorial
Commemorating the victims of state terror

South Africa's stability since 1994 is all the more admirable considering the extreme brutality of the preceding apartheid regime. The African National Congress (ANC), not wanting to remain defenseless against the government's troops, which were armed to the teeth, had also used weapons, aiming to destabilize the regime. The big, seemingly cool sculptures of the Seven Memorial in Gugulethu township commemorate that bloodstained period and the deadly dramas in the slums. By sunlight, the figures of the seven ANC activists shot down in Gugulethu in 1986 look alive and fleeting at the same time – an impressive work of art created by the South-African artists Donovan Ward and Paul Hendricks in 2005.

The memorial – located on one of the sites of the events of 1986 – recalls the fact that the Damocles sword of a terrible civil war overshadowed South Africa for many years. Even Nelson Mandela, who succeeded in implementing his vision of national reconciliation in the end, was no pacifist. He vehemently defended the use of weapons. The turning point for the ANC was the Sharpeville massacre in 1960, when security forces perpetrated a bloodbath upon unarmed demonstrators. Mandela personally then became the leader of the armed wing of the ANC, *Umkhonto we Sizwe* (Spearhead of the Nation), which attacked mainly police stations, military barracks, and government buildings. The state reacted with harshness and new strategies. *Agents provocateurs* infiltrated a group in Gugulethu, incited them to attack a police bus, and furnished them with weapons. On March 3, 1986, the attempt turned out to be a trap for the 16- to 23-year-old ANC fighters. They were encircled by two dozen police officers and riddled with bullets. The fact that not a single ANC man survived aroused skepticism even then.

Address Intersection of NY 1 (Steve Biko Drive) and NY 111, Gugulethu, Cape Town 7750 | **Getting there** By car: take N2 in the direction of Somerset West, exit 15, turn right on M10 (Duinefontein Road), turn left at the first intersection on M18 (Klipfontein Road), then left on Steve Biko Street. By public transit: Metrorail blue line, Heideveld station | **Hours** Viewable anytime, preferably by daylight | **Tip** Just a few hundred yards farther down Steve Biko Road is the Amy Biehl Memorial, a stone commemorating the U.S. student and human rights activist, who was murdered in 1993 by a black mob in Gugulethu because she was white.

86 __ The Shark Monument
Mobile high-tech sculpture

Sharks are a big subject on the Cape. Many beaches have shark warning flags blowing in the wind, their color signifying the current danger level. There are shark-related accidents along the coast almost every season, sometimes with a fatal ending for divers, surfers, or swimmers. The dreaded Great Whites, in particular, are also a tourist attraction: courageous divers are dropped into the water in cages, and then fish bait is thrown out, luring the animals into the shallows.

Shark researchers and animal welfare activists concerned with protecting this big fish, which is considered vulnerable to extinction, work at institutes and organizations in the Cape region. The most innocuous way of confronting this subject is to visit the unusual installation in the middle of Cape Town.

Since 2007, five skeletal shark sculptures have been hovering 10 feet above Jetty Square – a small, quiet, and – despite its painted pavements – not particularly attractive plaza. On commission by the city, the South-African artist Ralph Borland created this installation, which embodies the connection between city and nature, man and animal. The sculptures are blown about by the wind, and seem to be swimming in the air. This technically complex work of art is also interactive: if you approach one of the sharks, the metal fish moves in the direction of the wind, thanks to a sensitive infrared transmitter in the animal's nose, and you will hear a flutelike tone, the intensity of which depends on the velocity of the wind. The artwork is meant to remind visitors that at least part of the ground on which the city was built was snatched from an underwater world. Where the metal sharks hover today, real fish once swam hardly more than a half century ago. In the 1960s and 1970s, the bay was filled in to gain land for the growing metropolis.

Address 12 Jetty Street, City, Cape Town 8001 | **Getting there** By public transit: Bus 101/104/106/107, CTICC stop; "Hop on-Hop off" bus, CTICC stop | **Tip** The Save Our Seas Foundation (SOSF) Shark Education Centre, in Kalk Bay, offers information and events on the subject of sharks (www.saveourseas.com).

87 — Signal Hill
Flying high above the city

Signal Hill, 1150 feet high, was the vantage point in the 17th century for sighting ships approaching Cape Town Bay. Whenever frigates showed up, a signal was given from here. This was mainly for the benefit of the town's merchants and innkeepers, so they could get ready for business.

Today, Signal Hill, accessible without difficulty by car, is a favorite place for enjoying a divinely beautiful sunset over Cape Town. You can make yourself comfortable at small permanently installed tables, or on blankets on the grass, and take in a panorama that includes Table Bay up to Robben Island and Table Mountain. At nightfall, the view offers a practically endless sea of lights.

Signal Hill is also a popular place for rituals and contemplation. The Evangelical Lutheran Church of Cape Town celebrates its Easter services here, for instance.

And there's another specialty on Signal Hill: it's a great place for gliding. Various providers have their little sales booths on the mountain, from which – whether with reservations or spontaneously – you can jump off in the direction of Sea Point. The paragliders with their kites take off from a gigantic tarpaulin spread out on a slight decline that acts as a kind of ramp.

Tandem paragliding is in great demand: you sit in front of a strictly licensed professional who steers the kite safely over trees and houses toward the sun at the landing spots near the beach. From there, customers are driven back to Signal Hill, if they so desire.

There is also tandem paragliding at Lion's Head – to which the ascent is somewhat more difficult as the last 1000 feet up to the conic lion's head, nearly 2200 feet high, must be climbed on foot.

Address Signal Hill, Cape Town 8001 | **Getting there** By car: take Buitengracht Street onto Kloof Nek Road to Signal Hill Road (at the corner of Tafelberg Road); then drive uphill for about 2 miles (various parking places are available) | **Hours** Preferably at sunset; Cape Town Tandem Paragliding is recommended, Tel +27/768922283 | **Tip** Halfway up Signal Hill, you'll find a square white building with a green cupola – a *kramat*, the grave of a Muslim cleric. The building is open to the public.

88 __ The "Ski Jump"
Expressway to nowhere

West Cape Province is a stronghold of the Democratic Alliance. The African National Congress rules the rest of South Africa. Helen Zille, the prime minister on the Cape, is proud of the fact that social services and infrastructure are better here than elsewhere in the country. But even in Cape Town there is evidence of embarrassing planning errors, such as the elevated Eastern Boulevard Highway, never finished and leading to nowhere, right in the middle of town. This abruptly ending highway on tall pillars is an architectural sin of the apartheid period, but it has never been torn down.

There are only two groups who enjoy this spectacular planning disaster: movie directors and advertisers use the highway for all kinds of dramatic, comical, or scurrilous film scenes and photo shoots. During the soccer championship in 2010, a gigantic *vuvuzela* (a South African blowing horn) was mounted here.

The construction of the road was halted in 1977 for rather obscure reasons. The official explanation was that the city had run out of money. Others claimed that there were fatal construction errors, and there was even a rumor afoot that a recalcitrant resident had refused to permit the building of a pillar on his lot.

When the cost of continuing construction was estimated recently, people were horrified by the sum of about 200 million euros. Demolition, however, would also be expensive. So the ski-jump street has stayed put and is repeatedly immortalized in films. Conspiracy theorists maintain that this was the intention from the beginning: to build an attractive stage set for Hollywood. At a recent ideas competition, engineering students suggested turning the ruin into a skateboard park, an artificial waterfall, or a garden with monuments.

Address Eastern Boulevard Highway, Cape Town 8000 (the completed expressway on the other side is called Nelson Mandela Boulevard today) | **Getting there** By car: park somewhere around the corner of Buitengracht Street and Strand Street. By public transit: Bus 105, Strand Street stop | **Tip** The Cape Town International Convention Center (CTICC), one of Africa's most modern meeting halls, is quite nearby, at Convention Square, 1 Lower Long Street.

89__Slangkop Point
The tallest cast-iron lighthouse on the Cape

You'll be rewarded with a fantastic panorama if you take the trouble to clamber up the Slangkop Point lighthouse's long spiral staircase to the glass dome. Acrophobes be warned: here at the top, nothing blocks the view from a height of just over 100 feet. Slangkop Point is situated in an almost untouched dune landscape where a well-kept boardwalk invites you to take a comfortable stroll.

About 100 years ago, Sir Francis Hely-Hutchinson, the governor of the Cape, ordered the construction of the lighthouse because many ships had been running aground, wrecked or otherwise sunk before the rocky Kommetjies coast. Hundreds of vessels were unable to round the continent's southern tip. Heavy weather and rough seas at the meeting point of the Atlantic and Indian Oceans, with their differing temperatures, meant death for thousands of seamen. Even today, the 50 or so lighthouses on South Africa's long coastlines are of enormous importance.

A sign above the entrance to the tower announces its planned inauguration year of 1914. Due to the chaos of World War I, however, construction wasn't completed until 1919. The tallest cast-iron lighthouse in South Africa was named Serpent's Head because the winding road to Kommetjie resembles a snake. Slangkop is still operating today, but it no longer needs three watchmen as it once did. Since 1979, every 30 seconds, four flashes, which can be seen from a distance of some 40 miles, have been sent automatically from the top of the tower out to sea. A naval officer oversees the technical facilities. Visitors are welcome – with a special permit couples may even get married under the glass dome. The spectacular location and the mighty iron tower have lured film crews from all over the world.

Address Slangkop Lighthouse, Lighthouse Road, Kommetjie, Cape Town 7976, Tel +27/217831717 | **Getting there** By car: from Cape Town take the N2 expressway in the direction of Somerset West, exit to M3, turn right on Steenberg Road, then left onto Ou Kaapse Weg, then right onto Kommetjie Road; in Kommetjie, turn right on Lighthouse Road | **Hours** Oct–Apr, daily 10am–3pm; May–Sep, Mon–Fri 10am–3pm | **Tip** You can run into the wrecks of sunken ships at many places on the Cape, but very few of them stick out of the water. The best place to find some remnants is at Olifantsbos Point, about 12 miles south of Kommetjie.

90 __ The Slave Church
Where slaves were forced to become Christians

Prior to the late 18th century, it was strictly forbidden to convert slaves to the Christian faith. In particular, Asian slaves – many of whom were Muslim scholars and members of educated classes who had opposed Dutch rule over their Indonesian homeland – were forced to feel the power that their masters, as Christians, had over them. This attitude changed toward the end of the 18th century, however, with the founding of the Protestant Missionary Society (protected by British rule) in 1799. The society built its own church on Long Street in 1804, which became known as the first official church for slaves who were converted to Christianity in Cape Town. One of the most important missionaries was Briton Robert Moffat (1795–1883). At that time, there were about 30,000 slaves and 65,000 other inhabitants on the Cape.

The English abolitionist movement pressured the masters on the Cape as well. Slavery was officially abolished in 1806, but emancipation wasn't really enforced until 1833. Nonetheless, a system of compulsory labor was maintained by law on the Cape, the legacy of which brutalizes its society to this day. The Boers, for their part, migrated to the north and into the interior, founded their own republics, and upheld slavery, even using their Calvinistic faith to rationalize it.

The Slave Church is still considered Cape Town's oldest church. On the inside, everything is just as it was: the gallery of Ionic columns, the Chinese Chippendale pulpit, and the Ladegast organ from Germany, installed in 1903 after thorough renovation. The columns at the entrance are made of old ships' masts. Today, the Slave Church contains a small museum of the South African Missionary Society on the history of proselytizing in South Africa.

Address Slave Church Museum, 40 Long Street, City, Cape Town 8001, Tel +27/214236755 | Getting there By public transit: Bus 101, Mid Long Street stop; "Hop on-Hop off" bus, Long Street Tour Office stop | Hours Mon–Fri 9am–4pm | Tip Long Street, more than 300 years old, with its many restored Victorian-style houses and lots of shops, pubs, and restaurants, makes for a lovely stroll.

91 South Africa's Hollywood
A hotbed for filmmaking

As you drive on the N2 expressway from Cape Town in the direction of Somerset West over a comparatively flat landscape with lots of meadows, sand, and shrubs, a gigantic old pirate ship with mast and crow's nest suddenly pops up on your left – and then another one, at the end of a large wheat field. These are reconstructed originals from another epoch serving here as stage sets for one of the most successful television series ever made in South Africa: the U.S. pirate adventure series *Black Sails*, set in the Caribbean in 1720.

Here, at the edge of the Cape Flats, not far from Khayelitsha Township, are the Cape Town Film Studios, which opened in 2008. The complex comprises four gigantic 50-foot-tall numbered soundstages; two workshop buildings; production offices; and a variety of other facilities and open spaces, located in a 500-acre area.

It is a 40-million-euro project funded by international private investors and the regional government of the Western Cape. Two big international film productions are planned for the studio annually. In the long run, 10,000 new jobs are to be created.

For years, Cape Town Film Studios has been booked by photographers and producers in the advertising industry, but has recently also become increasingly popular with major filmmakers, who recognize the distinct advantages of the studio's unique location and state-of-the-art facilities. South Africa's spring and summer, from October to April, guarantee optimum weather and unique lighting opportunities. The studio provides excellent stage sets situated between gigantic mountainous regions and picturesque coastlines, as well as highly modern technology with comparatively economical production conditions. The new African film business is attracting more and more international directors and producers, and developing into a lucrative local industry.

Address Cape Town Film Studios, corner of Baden Powell Drive and N 2 Highway, Faure, Cape Town 7131, Tel +27/218432400, www.capetownfilmstudios.co.za | **Getting there** By car: take N2 to Baden Powell Drive exit (R 310); coming from Stellenbosch, to the right on R 310 | **Hours** The Cape Town Film Studios are expected to start offering tours to the public. A short excursion up to the gate is worthwhile even without a tour. | **Tip** Baden Powell Drive (R 310) leads to an attractive piece of coastline extending all the way to Muizenberg.

92 The Souvenir Garden
Life-sized mementos

If you come by car from Scarborough on A65 and turn from Red Hill Road onto Plateau Road, you'll run into two special kinds of animal compounds. Beneath shady trees in a sparse grove, you'll suddenly find yourself standing in front of gigantic fenced-in beasts: giraffes, mighty hippopotami, elephants with raised trunks, leopards, and zebra couples, all made out of wood and stone. There are also hundreds of sculptures with African motifs: humans, shamans, and other fantastic shapes – heads, busts, and even an armada of little elephants made of polished soapstone, all of them crafted individually. At the end of the grove, there is yet another collection of life-sized animals and people.

Here, at the roadside, a gigantic hodgepodge of souvenirs is on display – some of them kitschy, but others quite interesting. The big animals, costing up to 3,000 euros, are bought mainly by South Africans, while many of the smaller ones are sold to tourists. The vendors, with their offices in small green wooden huts standing on stilts, are ready to haggle over the prices, whether high or low.

Many of the artists and craftspeople are trained stonecutters who came to the new South Africa from Zimbabwe in the middle of the 1990s, bringing their skills and their own Zimbabwe Shona style with them. About ten unofficial dealers share the two sculpture gardens. Most of the pieces are produced and polished on the spot, in a little shack at the edge of the exhibit, or under a long corrugated tin roof, where the items are also protected from the rain.

For complex, particularly detailed sculptures, the stonecutters often need several weeks; but many pieces are also transported here from Zimbabwe.

Address Plateau Road, corner of Red Hill Road, Redhill, Cape Town 7975, Tel +27/21780127 | **Getting there** By car: take Red Hill Road (M65) from Scarborough, or Plateau Road from the Cape; entrance at Cape Farm House Restaurant | **Hours** Daily 10am–5pm | **Tip** Red Rock Tribal (watch for the sign), a shop purveying works by Pan-African artists (www.redrocktribal.co.za), is nearby. Also, some of the best and lowest-priced South African arts and crafts are sold along the roadside, often by people from the townships.

93 Straight No Chaser
Feel the beat of Cape Town's jazz scene

Cape Town is the jazz capital of Southern Africa – as shown by the annual jazz festival that usually takes place in March, and by the numerous jazz joints in the "Mother City." This is where the great old master Abdullah Ibrahim is at home, often giving concerts in the city of his birth. Straight No Chaser, with its 55 table seats and dozens of bar stools, is one of the smaller and more intimate jazz clubs in town. "For the artists, by the artists," is the motto of the establishment, which opened in 2014 directly next to Cape Town's oldest pub, Perseverance Tavern (built in 1808). In contrast to its predecessor, the Mahagony Room, the repertoire at Straight No Chaser has been expanded to include blues and electronic music.

Named after the eponymous song, the club is ambitiously modeled after such famed establishments as the Village Vanguard and Smalls in New York, and Ronnie Scott's in London. Though it may still be a while before the local venues in Cape Town are mentioned in the same breath as these classics of the international jazz scene, the two founders of Straight No Chaser – drummer Kesivan Naidoo and trumpeter Lee Thomson – have attained a very good reputation with their stage, on which mainly local young avant-garde musicians play – and this despite huge competition on the Cape. In the inner city alone, there are plenty of other established venues, such as the unusual Crypt Jazz Restaurant in the basement vault of Saint George's Cathedral, the musically varied Piano Bar in the De-Waterkant Quarter, and the intimate Studio 7 in Sea Point. The extent to which Cape Town's artistic scene has claimed this little jazz joint in the Gardens District as its own is also demonstrated by the events organized by filmmakers and writers on the evenings when there are no concerts.

Address Straight No Chaser Club, 79 Buitenkant Street, Gardens, Cape Town 8001, Tel +27/766792697, www.straightnochaserclub.wordpress.com | **Getting there** By public transit: Bus 103, Roodehek Street stop | **Hours** Tue–Sat starting at 7pm, shows at 8:30pm & 10:30pm | **Tip** Asoka, at 68 Kloof Street, a half mile away, offers live jazz on Tuesdays and Thursdays, as well as excellent Asian cuisine under Cape Town's oldest olive tree. In the summer, the roof of the old Victorian town house is partially opened (Tel +27/214220909).

94 The Synagogue
Jewish life on the Cape

When the British took power and established religious freedom in 1806, the first sizable group of European Jews came to South Africa. Most of them settled on the Cape. Tikvath Israel, the first Jewish congregation in Cape Town, was founded as early as 1841. Starting in 1860, in the wake of the diamond and gold rush, more and more Jews immigrated to South Africa, mainly from England and Germany, to seek their fortune. South Africa's first synagogue was built in 1863 in Company's Garden. Today, it is the foyer of the modern Jewish Museum, which, after thorough modernization, was ceremoniously reopened in 2000 by Nelson Mandela.

Between 1880 and 1910, around 40,000 Jews from Eastern Europe moved to South Africa, mainly due to anti-Semitism in their homelands. Today, the largest part of Cape Town's Jewish community is of Lithuanian descent. The Great Synagogue with its imposing dome was built in 1905. Starting in 1933, thousands of Jews fled to Cape Town to escape Nazi terror. But with the so-called Aliens Act, the South African government, which sympathized with Nazi Germany, strictly limited immigration. The Cape Town Holocaust Centre documents the horrors of Nazi Germany and World War II.

Through state-of-the-art interactive technology, the Jewish Museum presents the history of South-African Jews and their influence on political, cultural, and economic life. Jews were leading craftspeople and builders, played a prominent role in the gold and diamond business, founded big daily newspapers, and dominated the wool industry and ship construction. Many Jews fought against the apartheid regime, which was also openly anti-Semitic, and many of them were active in the opposition party, the African National Congress (ANC).

Address Great Synagogue, South African Jewish Museum, and Cape Town Holocaust Centre, 88 Hatfield Street, Gardens, Cape Town 8001, Tel +27/214651546, www.sajewishmuseum.co.za (Museum), Tel +27/214625553, www.holocaust.org.za (Holocaust Centre) | **Getting there** By public transit: Bus 101/103, Annandale stop; "Hop on-Hop off" bus, SA Jewish Museum stop | **Hours** Sun–Thu 10am–5pm, Fri 10am–2pm (identification necessary for the security check at the entrance) | **Tip** Right next door, you should definitely visit the National Gallery. Cape Town's biggest auction house for art and antiques is also close by, at Vrede Street 8.

95 The Taal Monument
Monument to the Afrikaans language

The Taal Monument, on the southern slopes of Paarl Mountain, is visible from everywhere in the valley below. Designed by architect Jan van Wijk (1926–2005) in 1975, it commemorates the origins of the independent Afrikaans language born a hundred years earlier in Paarl, which was declared South Africa's second official language after English in 1925. The Boers saw Afrikaans as the symbol of their own culture on the Cape. But Afrikaans also stood for suppression and apartheid. In Paarl, the *Afrikaanse Patriot*, the first newspaper in the new language, was printed.

The abstract monument consists of steles, columns, and arches of varying heights – the tallest one (187 feet) stands for Afrikaans. The language developed as a mixture of Dutch, French, German, and English, as well as the African languages Khoisan and Xhosa, and the Malayan-Indonesian influence of the slaves kidnapped to the Cape. Afrikaans enjoyed a great impetus when the British wanted to elevate English to the status of the sole official language in 1828, which aroused virulent protest. After the abolition of slavery led to the "Great Trek" (1835–1841) of the Boers into the territories north of the Oranje River, and to the founding of the *Zuid-Afrikaansche Republiek* (South African Republic), only Afrikaans was spoken there. In the end, Afrikaans was proclaimed a language all its own on August 14, 1875.

From the Taal Monument – *taal* means "language" in Afrikaans – you'll be able to see for miles over the vast agricultural region of the Paarl Valley, and the adjoining mountain ranges. The views are dramatic. The monument is surrounded by an enchanting park. Concerts are given regularly on the lawn – from rock to jazz.

Address Gabbema Doordrift, Paarl 7646, Tel +27/218634809, www.taalmonument.co.za |
Getting there By car: Take N 1 onto R 45; it will be on your left-hand side | **Hours**
April–Nov, daily 8am–5pm, Dec–Mar, daily 8am–8pm | **Tip** There is further
information in the visitors' center at the monument. You can deepen your insight into
the history of Afrikaans in the Taalmuseum on Pastorie Avenue in Paarl.

96 __ The Test Kitchen

A little restaurant with a great reputation

Africa's ostensibly best restaurant – and the 48th best in the whole world, according to the famous San Pellegrino List – is hidden in the back corner of the Old Biscuit Mill. The Test Kitchen has enhanced the value of this former cookie factory, the center of urban life in Woodstock. Among the cafes, bars, galleries, boutiques, delicatessens, and antiques shops here, this exquisite restaurant lures clientele of all types. So if you want to dine in this tasteful, somewhat austerely decorated restaurant, you'll have to make your reservation weeks, if not months, in advance.

Chef Luke Dale-Roberts, recipient of many awards, made the Test Kitchen the focus of a world-famous culinary cult in the blink of an eye. At first sight, the team in the sparkling kitchen – which can be viewed from the outside – signals that you're in an absolutely top restaurant.

British-born Dale-Roberts, who can boast of already having cooked for Madonna and Kylie Minogue, dedicates himself to creative crossover cuisine, courageously combining tuna sashimi with Italian cheese toast, foie gras with meringue and fruits, or sweetbreads with falafel. The cooks here prepare lobster or kudu filet as masterfully as they do pork belly or marinated fish.

The renowned restaurant boasts one advantage characteristic of Cape Town: to enjoy this caliber of food in Berlin, London, or Vienna, you'd have to pay twice as much and more. Even the prices on the fastidiously composed wine list are moderate. Many first-class vintages can be ordered by the glass. Dale-Roberts wants to make his haute cuisine accessible to a wider circle of patrons in every respect, from using unpretentious waiters to offering an affordable menu. "Fine food for the people, by the people," he jests.

Address The Test Kitchen, Shop 104 A, The Old Biscuit Mill, 375 Albert Road, Woodstock, Cape Town 7915 | **Getting there** By car: take Strand Street onto R 102 (Newmarket Street), which turns into Albert Road. By public transit: Bus 102 to Woodstock, Kent Street stop | **Hours** Tue – Sat 12pm – 2pm & 7pm – 9pm | **Tip** Just a few yards away from the Test Kitchen, chocolate candies and truffles are made and sold in the small chocolate factory CocoáFair.

97 — The Theatre on the Bay
Where the avant-garde crowds together

In a city like Cape Town, with two dozen stages, small private theaters often have a hard time continually attracting their audiences, but the Theatre on the Bay has succeeded in this regard since 1988. The district of Camps Bay is particularly popular because of its lovely beaches and illustrious amusement quarter, and its theater is an integral part of Cape Town's cultural life. This private theater flourishes, above all, thanks to the passion and the capabilities of its producer and manager, Pieter Toerien. As a 20-year-old fledgling impresario, he had already managed to lure Hollywood legend Marlene Dietrich to South Africa. In 1964, he simply sat down in front of the door of her house until the singer and actress finally gave in and agreed to tour South Africa.

Toerien's successful concept for the 260-seat theater in Camps Bay is to offer diversity and variety. Dramas, musicals, and ballet are as much at home here as cabaret and stand-up comedy. The spectrum of productions ranges from such international stage hits as Andrew Lloyd Webber's *Sunset Boulevard* to the works of South-African playwrights and relatively unknown dramatists. Toerien habitually hires the popular satirist Pieter-Dirk Uys, who operates his famous transvestite theater in the Darling District, for gigs at the "Beach Theater." They share a fierce opposition to apartheid, a strong social commitment, and enthusiasm for lively and courageous theatrical art.

The Capetonians esteem the intimacy of Theatre on the Bay, in which actors often mingle with visitors in the lobby or at the bar after the performances. The theater's restaurant attracts customers with its multi-course dinners before the shows. Visitors from abroad may find it somewhat novel that they are permitted to take their drinks with them into the auditorium.

Address Theatre on the Bay, 1A Link Street, Camps Bay, Cape Town 8005, Tel +27/214383301, www.theatreonthebay.co.za | **Getting there** By car: take M6 in the direction of Sea Point, Clifton, and Camps Bay; all the way through the district, and almost at its end, turn left on Link Street. By public transit: Bus 106/108/109, Whale Rock stop | **Hours** Depending on the event, usually 8pm; Sundays often at 3pm | **Tip** Directly across the street, you'll find Camps Bay Tidal Pool, which contains seawater warmed by the sun. The beach at Camps Bay is in a class of its own.

98 The Toboggan Park
Downhill thrills for all ages

There's only one toboggan run in all of Africa: for this reason, Cool-Runnings Toboggan Park in Bellville lures not only tourists, but also many locals. On a lovely Saturday, there are sometimes more than 600 visitors. The .75-mile-long stainless steel track with 17 curves, double bends, and small tunnels is a construction from Germany. It was built in 1976 by Wiegand in Rasdorf near Fulda, which has been exporting ski lifts, slides, and tracks all over the world for decades. Cool-Runnings' operator is Toboggan Family Park, which is owned by German businessman Frank Unger.

Tobogganing is as easy as pie: the speed can be regulated with a simple servo hand brake, according to your taste and your gumption. Maximum speed is 25 miles per hour; more than four sleds are never underway at the same time. The sleds are automatically decelerated when entering the docking station. The sleds have double-seats for couples; children under eight have to sit with an adult.

The toboggan run is set very prettily into the park landscape, and a large roofed terrace facing the track is used year-round for all kinds of festivities. Kids celebrate their birthdays, and school classes meet here. Parents can relax with a pleasant picnic while the toboggan run's personnel watch over their children. A local snack bar offers a small selection of foods and drinks.

Young people are getting together to party here more and more often. The loudspeakers broadcast music all day long, and whenever a sizable group overtakes the run, they can decide what music is to be played, whether hip-hop or hard rock. As the number of visitors over 18 has been growing steadily for years, the toboggan run is now open occasionally in the evening.

Address Cool-Runnings Toboggan Park, Carl Cronje Drive, Bellville, Cape Town 7530, Tel +27/219494439, www.cool-runnings.co.za | **Getting there** By car: from Cape Town take N1 in the direction of Paarl for about 15 miles to exit 23, turn left on Willem van Schoor Avenue, then onto Mispel Road; at the intersection with Carl Cronje Drive, go straight ahead to the entrance to Cool-Runnings; the complex is directly across from Bellville Velodrom | **Hours** Tue–Fri 11am–6pm, weekends and holidays 9am–6pm, closed when it rains | **Tip** In case sudden rain stops you from visiting the toboggan run, the reptile garden in Stodels Garden Centre on Eversdal Road is an interesting alternative in Bellville.

99 The Treadmill
Instrument of torture at Breakwater Lodge

Racism lorded over many aspects of South African society long before apartheid became the country's official political system in 1948. Back in the 19th century, Breakwater Prison was already strictly segregated. Despite certain privileges for white prisoners, however, this prison was a chamber of horrors for all of its inmates. The "treadmill," installed in 1890, still bears witness to the horrific treatment of those who were incarcerated here. It was an instrument of torture used to torment up to three prisoners simultaneously. Whoever became too exhausted to run fell with his limbs into the gears. Terrible bruises or fractures were the result.

The premises now harbors the Protea Hotel Breakwater Lodge and the University of Cape Town's Graduate School of Business. However, the four corner towers, and some of the original buildings, walls, and installations of the prison are preserved. The personnel of the hotel are usually happy to show tourists the gruesome equipment. En route, you can see the barely decipherable scribblings, slogans, and drawings made by the prisoners on the walls. In the halls of the hotel, there are old registers under glass, listing minutely and pedantically the delinquents, their crimes, their punishments, and the dates.

Erected in 1859, Breakwater Prison was mainly used by the British colonial masters as a repository for deported convicts from the mother country. The Capetonians protested in vain against the importing of dangerous felons. The inmates of the prison right next to the ocean were used to expand the harbor, being forced to work on dam and street construction, and in the mines.

While the prisoners feared the treadmill, it wasn't used very often. The need for strong workers ready for action on the innumerable construction sites was too great.

Address Protea Hotel Breakwater Lodge, Portswood Road on the V&A Waterfront, Cape Town 8001, Tel +27/214061911 | **Getting there** By public transit: Bus 104, Nobel Square stop; "Hop on-Hop off" bus, Aquarium stop | **Hours** Always accessible, recommended in daylight; the treadmill is also a part of the daily Waterfront Historic Walking Tours starting at Chavonnes Battery Breakwater Museum | **Tip** In Chavonnes Battery Breakwater Museum in the Waterfront Center, you can see 18th-century weapons and get information on the battles around Cape Town (The Clock Tower Precinct).

100 _ The Tree Walkway
Tiptoeing through the treetops

For more than a century now, the Kirstenbosch National Botanical Garden (NBG) has been attracting natives and tourists with its splendid walkways through dense woods and well-tended gardens, its breathtaking view of Table Mountain, and its enormous abundance of plants and blossoms. Every year, around 700,000 visitors flock to this picturesque reserve, donated to the state by entrepreneur and politician Cecil Rhodes shortly before his death in 1902.

Since 2014, visitors have been able to study the Cape's fauna and flora from a new perspective: the Centenary Tree Canopy Walkway, a 425-foot-long boardwalk through the tops of the trees, some of which are quite ancient. The view from the walkway across the vast park landscape below Table Mountain, and over Table Bay in front of Cape Town and the northern suburbs, is overwhelming.

Boomslang ("tree serpent") is the Capetonians' nickname for this fascinating construction made of wood and steel. The occasionally swaying elevated boardwalk wends its way in a semicircle at airy heights among and above treetops, providing an exciting proximity to the exotic birds in this natural paradise. With great virtuosity, the architects have integrated the steel elements of the walkway with the dense growth found in this part of the garden. Near the Protea Garden, the Boomslang is even wheelchair accessible.

You can walk for many hours on Kirstenbosch's more than 9 miles of well-groomed paths, which are full of great variety. There are frequent exhibitions of the works of young South African artists here, and for those more interested in an athletic challenge, the Botanical Garden is also an idyllic departure point for hikes into the conservation area leading up to Table Mountain.

Address Kirstenbosch National Botanical Garden, Rhodes Drive, Newlands, Cape Town 7735, Tel +27/217998783, www.sanbi.org/gardens/kirstenbosch | **Getting there** By car: From Cape Town via M3, Kirstenbosch exit. By public transit: Golden Arrow bus, Mowbray-Kirstenbosch line, Kirstenbosch stop; "Hop on-Hop off" bus, Kirstenbosch stop | **Hours** Sep–March, daily 8am–7pm; April–Aug, daily 8am–6pm | **Tip** Many well-groomed lawns invite you to have a picnic. A picnic basket can also be ordered from the Kirstenbosch Tea Room.

101_ The Turkish Bath
100 years of aquatic joy

Does a city surrounded by the ocean really need an indoor swimming pool? Probably not, but Cape Town has one, nonetheless. Though somewhat antiquated and tarnished, the century-old public pool at the end of Long Street is clean and functional, and well managed by the city.

Of course, such a pool (the only one of its kind in town) does make sense. For where else should aquatic athletes train during the South African winter? There are many swim teams on the Cape; the Walmers, the Cape Stormers, and the Trafalgar Club all train regularly at the Long Street pool during the week from 5pm to 7pm in the evening. Otherwise, the pool is open to all Capetonians – and many of them are business people who swim a few laps during their lunch break – at least during the summer. There's also a pool for kids and a sundeck.

The pool was built in 1908 – offering bathing facilities at the time for those unable to shower or bathe at home. In 1926, a Turkish bath was added as a supplement to the big swimming hall with its 25-meter pool, and was a great success from the start.

The facility now has two steam baths, a sauna, massage benches, a cold plunge pool, and showers. The sauna and the steam bath are separated by gender.

There was a preceding Turkish bath at this spot as early as 1860. Parts of the exterior walls of the swimming pool and the relaxation room of the steam bath are fantastically painted by artists unknown today.

The Turkish bath and the swimming hall offer an excellent place to retreat from the bustle of the city – during the morning or around noon, you might even have the place nearly all to yourself.

Address Long Street Baths, Orange Street on the corner of Long Street, Gardens, Cape Town 8001, Tel +27/214003302 | **Getting there** By public transit: Bus 101/106/107, Upper Long Street stop; "Hop on-Hop off" bus, South African Museum stop | **Hours** Swimming pool: daily 7am–7pm. It's advisable to call in advance to ask whether the Turkish bath is operating. Sauna and steam bath: Mon, Thu & Sat for women; Tue, Wed, Fri, & Sun for men | **Tip** You'll find the Saint Martini Evangelical Lutheran Church of Cape Town diagonally across the street. The Jumu'a Mosque is right next door to the swimming-pool building.

102 The Underground Tunnels
Mysterious downtown underworld

If you book a tour through Cape Town's little-known subterranean tunnels, you should be prepared for a wet, sometimes rather inhospitable adventure, and dress accordingly. Above all, waterproof shoes and jackets are advisable. The reward for this undertaking will be unusual insights into the history of the metropolis gleaned during an underworld expedition led by expert guides.

As early as the mid-17th century, the first colonial rulers were using the abundance of water beneath Table Mountain to supply ships in the harbor by means of an open canal system. This is how such street names as Buitengracht (*grachten* is Dutch for "canals") came about. At that time, due to these many waterways, Cape Town was even called "Little Amsterdam." Under British government, however, the canals were closed at the end of the 19th century to make room for streets and houses.

Today, two agencies offer one- to three-hour tours through the complicated underground system. The small groups usually start by clambering down a nondescript shaft outside the walls of the Castle of Good Hope. Participants lift the lid of a manhole and equipped with helmets, headlamps, and rubber boots, climb down iron rungs. The destination of the expedition is usually an exit at a higher place in the Gardens District. At present, the catacombs are only a tourist attraction. However, an initiative called "Reclaim Camissa" (founded in 2010) advocates the use of the natural abundance of water to supply the city. This would make Cape Town less dependent on water from distant springs. Cape Town's original inhabitants belonging to the San tribe called the area at the foot of Table Mountain *Camissa* – "place of the sweet water" – because of its numerous brooks fed by 36 springs.

Address Castle of Good Hope, Buitenkant Street, City, Cape Town 8001 | **Getting there** By public transit: Bus 102, Castle stop; "Hop on-Hop off" bus, Castle of Good Hope stop | **Hours** Tours upon reservation during the day or evening through Good Hope Adventures, www.goodhopeadventures.com, or Teambuilding Figure of 8, www.fo8.co.za | **Tip** In the Dragon Room club at 84 Harrington Street, the dance floor is underground in a catacomb (Tel +27/214618701).

103 Vergelegen Wine Farm
The wine farm and slavery

Tradition is trump at Vergelegen Wine Farm. After all, the picturesque estate, whose name means "remote" in Afrikaans, has been cultivating grapes, fruit, and vegetables since 1685. Evidence of this 300-year history can be glimpsed throughout the elegant grounds. The foundation was laid by Willem Adriaan van der Stel, the Dutch governor of Cape Town, at the end of the 17th century. The former main building is a museum today. The precious furniture, the library, and the numerous oil paintings will give you an inkling of the noble lifestyle enjoyed by wealthy landowners on the Cape at that time.

But you will also be informed in detail about the dark side of this splendor. Pictures, wall charts, and documents describe the role of the slaves – their unpaid labor and the wretched conditions they lived in – which made the luxury, beauty, and success of the estate possible to begin with.

Now under U.S. ownership, Vergelegen is near Helderberg in the middle of the winegrowing region, a less than 40-minute drive from Cape Town. Nobody would find this terribly "remote" today. It is a favorite destination for excursions for many Capetonians. Thanks to this popularity, the proprietors levy a small admission fee.

The capacious, immaculately kept park, with its more than 300-year-old avenue of camphor trees, its lush rose and camellia gardens, and its painstakingly trimmed lawns and hedges, is an ideal setting for a picnic. Baskets, including the house's award-winning wines, such as Vergelegen Red or Vergelegen V, are available in the restaurant.

Live music concerts – mainly classical – are also given here. In 2008, pop star Céline Dion performed before several thousand spectators.

Address Vergelegen Estate, Lourensford Road, Somerset West, Cape Town 7130, Tel +27/218471334, www.vergelegen.co.za | **Getting there** By car: take N2 in the direction of Somerset West, Victoria Street exit, then turn left on Main Road, then right on Lourensford Road. By public transit: Metrorail green line, Somerset West Station, and then about another 50 minutes on foot | **Hours** Daily 9:30am–5pm (admission only until 4pm); Camphors restaurant is open until 9pm | **Tip** Morgenster olive plantation next door to Vergelegen offers interesting olive and oil tastings.

104__ Waterkloof
The restaurant in a giant glass cube

You can argue about its beauty, but not about its originality: Waterkloof Wine Estate's restaurant is certainly one of the most unique in the region. The imposing edifice made of glass and concrete with its modern wine cellars deep in its belly nestles against the slope of Schaapenberg, overgrown with fynbos. The modern architecture is astonishing. In this wine region with its Cape Dutch-style manors, the building looks like a futuristic foreign body. When the vineyard was given over to its owners in 2009, the locals called it the "James Bond Estate."

But the concept is convincing: in the face of the enormous competition of picturesque wine farms, Waterkloof will impress you with a courageously contrasting aesthetic, with excitingly designed dining rooms in which first-class French and South-African style cuisines are served, the preparation of which can be observed in the open kitchen. If you come only for a wine tasting and hors d'oeuvres, you'll find modern black armchairs and sofas at rather rustic wooden tables surrounding a circular open fireplace. Visitors to the restaurant in the glass cube enjoy a fantastic panorama all the way to False Bay. Works of art from renowned galleries such as the Everard Read Gallery in Cape Town are continuously exhibited here.

Waterkloof was designed by Australian architect Mitch Hayhow. The building, with its 32-foot-high glass walls, is meant to reflect the philosophy of the biodynamic wine farm, which advertises itself with the slogan, "Honesty, transparency, and authenticity." The vintners emphasize that they use no chemical sprays, mechanical harvesters, or preservatives. South-African architect Frank Bohm succeeded in designing an unusual interior with large hand-lathed copper lamps and a fireplace flickering cozily even in the summertime.

Address Waterkloof Wine Estate, Old Sir Lowry's Pass Road, Somerset West, Cape Town 7129, Tel +27/218581491, www.waterkloofwines.co.za | **Getting there** By car: take expressway N 2 to Somerset West; after reaching the town, turn left on Main Road, and at the end of the street, turn right on Old Sir Lowry's Pass Road | **Hours** Open year-round (except for June 16 – July 16). Oct – Apr, Mon – Sat 12 – 4pm & 7 – 9pm, Sun 12 – 2pm; May – Sept, Wed – Sat 12 – 2pm and 7 – 9pm, Sun 12 – 2pm | **Tip** You can see demonstrations of eagles and other birds of prey at Spier Vineyard, Spier Estate, on Lynedoch Road (R 310) in Stellenbosch (www.eagle-encounters.co.za).

105 _ The White Circle
The center of the city

The center of the city is at Greenmarket Square – directly in front of the Old Town House, to be precise – Cape Town's first city hall. On the small outdoor veranda of the two-story house built between 1755 and 1761 in the so-called Cape Rococo style, with its columned porch, its three distinctive entrance arches, and its artistically decorated bell tower, an easily visible white circle is set into the floor, surrounded by reddish brown stones laid out in the manner of a mosaic. Starting at this point, the area was to be surveyed, and the distances to points in the city and into the hinterland were to be established. Though the function of the white circle is not historically documented, for connoisseurs of Cape Town's history, there is no doubt that the circle was set into the floor in 1761 for this reason. On the other hand, you will search in vain for a sign concerning any of this information.

Standing on this spot in front of the entrance to the Old Town House, you're on doubly historic terrain. For the Old Town House was the city's first public building, and its city hall until 1905. It lost this function with the construction of the Victorian-style city hall on Grand Parade, the former military parade grounds. Since 1916, the Old Town House has been a place of culture. It harbors a collection of great Dutch and Flemish masters of the 17th century, with works by Anton van Dyck and Frans Hals, which were donated to the city in 1914 by Sir Max Michaelis, and is supplemented by steadily changing exhibitions.

In the idyllic inner courtyard of the building there stands a bust of the banker of German origin who founded this art collection. There is also a cozy cafe here, an oasis of reflection on the otherwise rather hectic Greenmarket Square.

Address Old Town House, Greenmarket Square, City, Cape Town 8000, Tel +27/214813933, www.iziko.org.za | **Getting there** By car: take Long Street or Adderley Street between Longmarket and Shortmarket Streets. By public transit: Bus 101, Longmarket stop; "Hop on-Hop off" bus, Long Street Tour Office stop | **Hours** Mon–Sat 10am–5pm | **Tip** The two monuments to Jan van Riebeeck and his wife Maria are located where Adderley turns into Heerengracht Street.

106 — Wilderer Distillery
The masters of grappa

There are many vineyards around Cape Town – a paradisiac condition for anyone who loves wine tastings outdoors. But if you're looking for a producer of choice liqueurs, spirits, schnapps, and brandies in this lush region of wine and fruit, you're surprisingly in for a hard time. Helmut Wilderer probably also found this odd when he decided to open his own distillery here. In the middle of the 1990s, Wilderer, who had thoroughly learned his trade in Germany and Austria, and had managed a good restaurant in the southwestern German region of Baden, immigrated to South Africa. His goal: manufacturing first-class schnapps and liqueurs, for the government's monopoly on making them had just fallen.

Wilderer received the first private license for a distillery in 1995. It was logical to concentrate on grape and pomace brandies in a wine-growing region – which meant grappa. This became the German craftsman's specialty, and Wilderer's grappas have attained renown far beyond the Cape region.

At first, he operated his distillery in Stellenbosch; in 2000, he moved to the wine-growing area of Paarl. His spirits have won him numerous international medals and awards. Besides the grappas made mainly from typically South-African Pinotage grapes, his various fruit brandies and Wilderer's Fynbos, a unique apertif made with more than 30 herbs from the Cape region, are particularly outstanding.

Together with his son Christian, he also operates his restaurant Pappa Grappa, next to his distillery near R45. In 2013, Wilderer opened a second restaurant on Spice Route Farm, also near Paarl. He imports the equipment for his high-tech distillery from Germany – from Kothe-Destillationstechnik in the federal state of Baden-Württemberg.

Address Wilderer Distillery, R 45, Simondium, Paarl 7670, Tel +27/218633555, www.wilderer.co.za | **Getting there** By car: take R 45 (wine route) nearly 2 miles outside Paarl in the direction of Franschhoek | **Hours** Tue – Sat 11:30am – 9pm, Sun 11:30am – 5pm | **Tip** Right next to Paarl Station, you'll find Kooperatiewe Wijnbouwers Vereeniging (KWV), the biggest South African wine cooperative, which was founded in 1918. Visiting the KWV's cellars with tours and wine tastings is definitely worthwhile.

107 _ The Wildlife Reservation
Africa's fauna not far from Cape Town

Cape Town isn't known as the best place to get close to South African fauna: there's no guarantee that you can find the "big five" – lions, elephants, rhinoceroses, buffalos, and leopards – running free here. Above all, hardly any of Cape Town's many beautiful wildlife parks can compete with the gigantic Kruger National Park in the northeastern part of the country. Nonetheless, one can still have an impressive experience of nature and animals near the city. For instance, hardly more than an hour's drive away, near Darling, you can visit Buffelsfontein Game & Nature Reserve in the savanna area.

Twice a day, safaris in sizable jeeps lasting three hours each are offered in the malaria-free wildlife park. On a "game drive" you stand a good chance of seeing giraffes, lions, zebras, antelopes, gnus, cheetahs, and ostriches. Experienced gamekeepers will inform you about the lifestyles of the wildlife. Some of the animals, however, don't live in freedom, but in compounds, and are lured to the fences with fodder.

The grounds, comprising about 4000 acres, used to be a cattle farm. In 1993 it was converted by a private South-African investor into a well-maintained tourist resort with a restaurant, comfortable accommodations, and a swimming pool – but with relatively few animals at the time, due to a shortage of security fences. During the hot summer of 2000, a devastating brushfire destroyed the facilities. But in a relatively short time, everything was rebuilt, and a large, attractive wildlife reservation was created. Today, it has small guesthouses in a bush camp picturesquely situated in the grassland. All of the quarters are close to watering holes where the animals come to drink at dawn and sunset.

Address Buffelsfontein Farm, West Coast Road, Darling 7345, Tel +27/224512824, www.sa-venues.com | **Getting there** By car: take R27; after Darling the exit is on the right-hand side; upon reservation, the wildlife park also organizes a shuttle service to the reservation and back | **Hours** Safaris at 9am & 2pm | **Tip** The Hildebrand Monument in Darling (Kraalbosdam Farm, Burgherspan Road) commemorates the battles between the Boers and the British in the Second Boer War – it was erected in 1939 for the Boer commander C. P. Hildebrand.

108 The Wine Route
Wine farms behind Table Mountain

Wines from Constantia Valley were already in great demand among Europe's high nobility centuries ago, and are still considered some of the country's best.

Not long after his arrival in 1652, Cape Town's founder Jan van Riebeeck realized that the mild Mediterranean climate and soil were excellent for wine growing. So he had grapevines imported. After initial setbacks, extensive vineyards were cultivated thanks to the Huguenots emigrating from France. Groot Constantia, which calls itself the country's oldest wine farm – a claim that doesn't go entirely uncontested – made its first impression with sweet wines. The cellarers of Napoleon were among their early customers. In 1833, the royal house of France bought up the entire vintage.

For Capetonians, the wine farms in Constantia are practically around the corner. By car, you only drive for 15 minutes to reach the gently curving hills south of Table Mountain. On the approximately 12.5-mile-long "Constantia Wine Route," consisting of several roads, there are ten wine farms that are almost all open for tastings. Although Groot Constantia receives more than 400,000 visitors each year, the vast area with its avenue of oak trees, Cape Dutch manor, museum, and two restaurants seldom seems overcrowded. You should reserve your table in the shady park in front of the Jonkerhuis restaurant in advance, however.

Uitsig Wine Farm advertises its comfortable guest house and its internationally renowned gourmet restaurant La Colombe. Steenberg Wine Farm boasts a five-star hotel with a spa; its parklike grounds are strewn with modern sculptures. Steenberg's restaurant is highly rated, as is the restaurant at elegant Buitenverwachting Wine Farm.

Address Groot Constantia, Groot Constantia Road, Cape Town 7806, wine route: www.constantiavalley.com/vineyards | Getting there By car: take M 3 in the direction of Muizenburg, Constantia exit. By public transit: "Hop on-Hop off" bus (Wine Tour of Constantia Valley) | Hours Major wine farms: 9am–6pm; restaurants until 10pm | Tip At Porter Estate Produce Market in the woods in the Tokai district, besides selling local products, arts and crafts, and unusual snacks, there are often live concerts given by local groups (Sat 9am–1pm, Chrysalis Academy Grounds, Porter Estate).

109 __ The Wine Tram

A historic tram ride through the wine region

Although the historic "Wine Tram" dating from 1890 isn't a party train, taking it is a pleasure trip. While no alcohol is served on board the picturesque railway vehicles, you can certainly relax between the seductive wine tastings as the tram chugs along leisurely through the pastoral scenery. In the airy, open big cars, the history and the unique qualities of South Africa's wine region are elucidated.

At the tram's individual stations, there's plenty of time to enjoy wine, culinary tidbits, or even a copious lunch. In addition to exquisite wine tastings at moderate prices, tours through the wine cellars are offered. Naturally, you can also just rest comfortably at the lovely, carefully kept farms with their typical Cape Dutch buildings.

At the ticket office of the Wine Tram, you'll have a choice between the blue and the red line, each of which visits a different group of vineyards. The "Hop on-Hop off" tours start between 10am and 1:30pm. They differ with regard to the duration and the number of stops. But all of the excursions go slowly and comfortably through the gently rolling wine farms of Franschhoek. The passengers can decide individually how long they stay at each stop. If you'd like to linger longer, you can just take the next bus or tram.

Along the tour, you'll immerse yourself in the wine farms founded mainly by the Huguenots who settled here 300 years ago, bringing their refined expertise in wine along with them from France.

The vineyards such as La Couronne and Moreson, or Leopard's Leap and Chamonix, all have excellent reputations. You can of course also buy the wines – at a discount, in fact, as a participant on the tour.

Address Bijoux Square, 60 Huguenot Street, Franschhoek 7690, Tel +27/213000338, www.winetram.co.za | **Getting there** By car: take N2, exit 47 to the right on R44, Adam Tass Street, then turn left on R45 to Franschhoek | **Hours** Tours 10am–1:30pm, office opens at 9am | **Tip** You can take lovely hikes in the seldom-visited Mont Rochelle Nature Reserve near Franschhoek.

110 The World Championship Stadium
The UFO that landed in Green Point

The stadium looks like a mysterious spaceship, with its festive illumination. Although it's a fascinating arena, the Capetonians don't like it. They never wanted it – not the neighbors, or the soccer fans, or the politicians.

Before the 2010 World Cup championship in Cape Town, FIFA refused to accept a redevelopment of old stadiums in less attractive neighborhoods: a new building would be necessary for the final rounds, it said. So the sensational arena was raised for four hundred million euros.

But everybody knew that the stadium, with its current 55,000 seats, would have enormous follow-up costs and be used much too seldom, for the soccer players of Ajax Cape Town and the members of the Stormers rugby team prefer to play in the traditional stadiums of the workers' quarter of Athlone or the suburb of Newlands. Big events in the new Cape Town Stadium take place only rarely, when Justin Bieber, Bon Jovi, U2, Coldplay, or Africa's biggest gay celebration attract the masses, for instance. Otherwise, the arena is pretty much a "white elephant."

The city fathers have been cudgeling their brains for years over how to compensate for the millions in deficits. The plan to create a gigantic shopping center with restaurants, bars, conference rooms, and offices in the stadium fell through. The Congress of South African Trade Unions made the provocative suggestion that the stadium – in the middle of an amusement quarter with expensive apartment houses and luxury hotels – be converted into cheap accommodations for the poor. Many people are in favor of simply tearing it down.

Address 1 Fritz Sonnenberg Road, Green Point, Cape Town 8051, Tel +27/214170120 | Getting there By car: take M5 (Helen Suzman Boulevard), turn right on the traffic circle, then left onto Fritz Sonnenberg Road. By public transit: Bus 106, Stadium stop, "Hop on-Hop off" bus, Green Point and Urban Park stops | Hours Several guided tours daily, each about 90 minutes long; a VIP lounge can be rented for private celebrations, birthdays, or weddings | Tip Right next door is Green Point Park Biodiversity Showcase Garden with picnic tables and an adventure playground. The Metropolitan Golf Club, with its attractive clubhouse, is on the side facing the ocean. Next to the stadium, you can take a glance into Fort Wyngard.

111 The Zip Zap
Integration in a playful way

The circus staged in the mighty 72 by 115-foot Zip Zap tent in the heart of Cape Town is rather on the small side. Even though the magicians, and trapeze and tightrope artists regularly lure both natives and tourists to events and private celebrations like children's birthdays, Zip Zap isn't a commercial operation, but rather a social institution.

It was founded by acrobats Laurence Estève and Brent van Rensburg in 1992 in order to inspire young people. While Zip Zap certainly also wants to discover and promote circus talents, its actual objective is to bring children from all social levels together in a playful fantasy-filled way. "We want to help them dare to make their dreams come true, and to live out the culture of peaceful coexistence," explain the founders.

Here, children and adolescents, some of them with difficult social backgrounds, learn the arts of clowns, jugglers, and acrobats in courses free of charge. Some of the 7- to 18-year-olds are also given medical assistance and are regularly informed about HIV, a major health threat in South Africa.

Homeless or disadvantaged kids find a contact point at Zip Zap. Some of them stay permanently: children without families live in Zip Zap shelters, visit neighboring schools, and can begin professional training as dancers, costume designers, and theater managers.

The operation is financed by private donors, businesses, and humanitarian organizations. The world-famous Cirque du Soleil also supports the project.

Zip Zap has distinguished itself with many professional successes. The Baker Boys, for instance, who trained here as clowns and acrobats, won the international circus prize in Monte Carlo in 2002.

Address Zip Zap Circus School, Founders Garden, Jan Smuts Street, City, Cape Town 8001, Tel +27/214218622, www.zip-zap.co.za | **Getting there** By car: from the center of the city take Adderley Street, then turn right on Hertzog Boulevard; take the second left on Civic Avenue, which turns into Jan Smuts Street. By public transit: Bus 101/104/106/107, Foreshore stop; "Hop on-Hop off" bus, Foreshore stop | **Hours** Irregular performances, Fri & Sat circus school for schoolchildren and adolescents, registration necessary | **Tip** Very close by, on Malan Street, stands the Artscape Theatre Center (Tel +27/214109800, www.artscape.co.za).

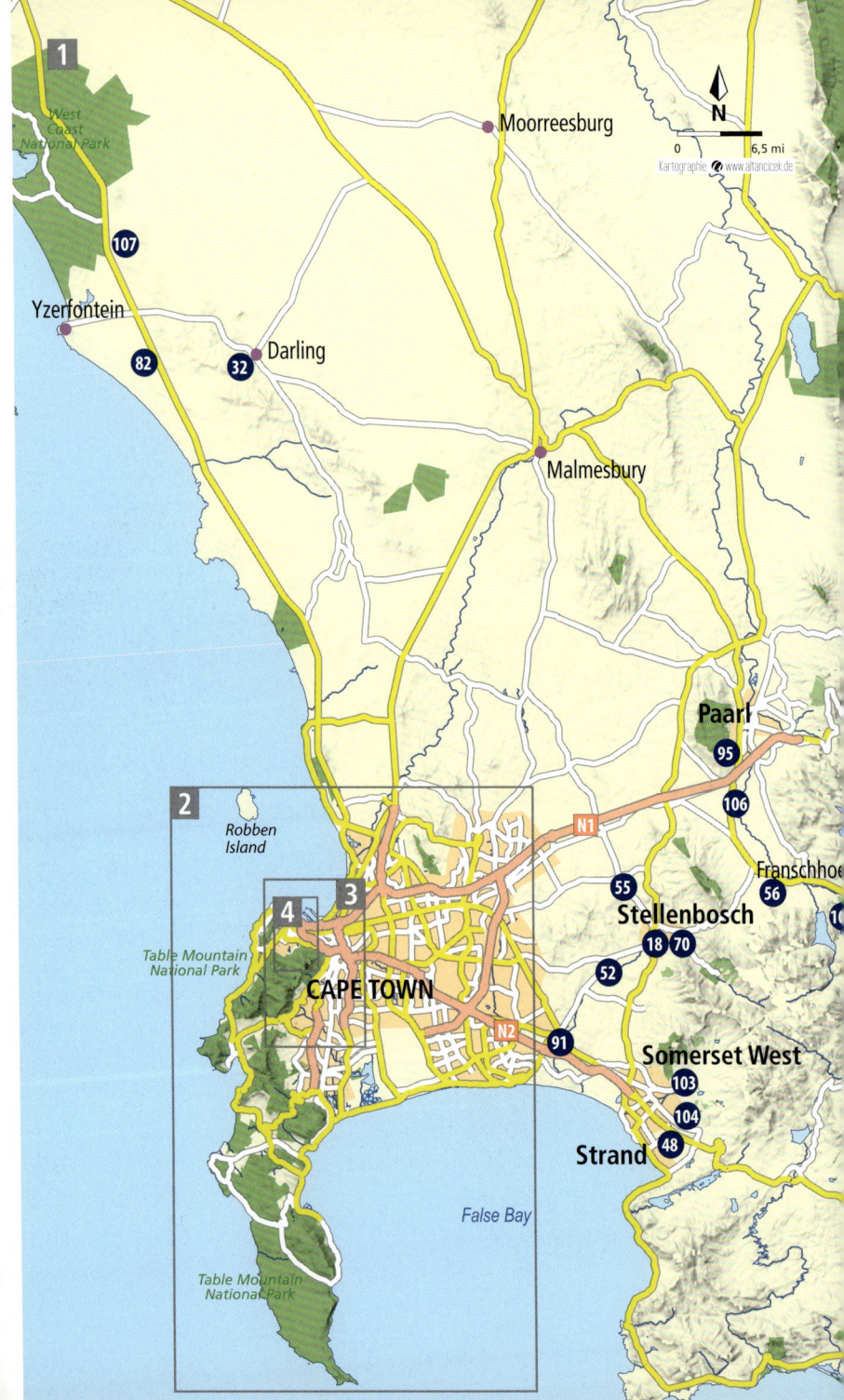

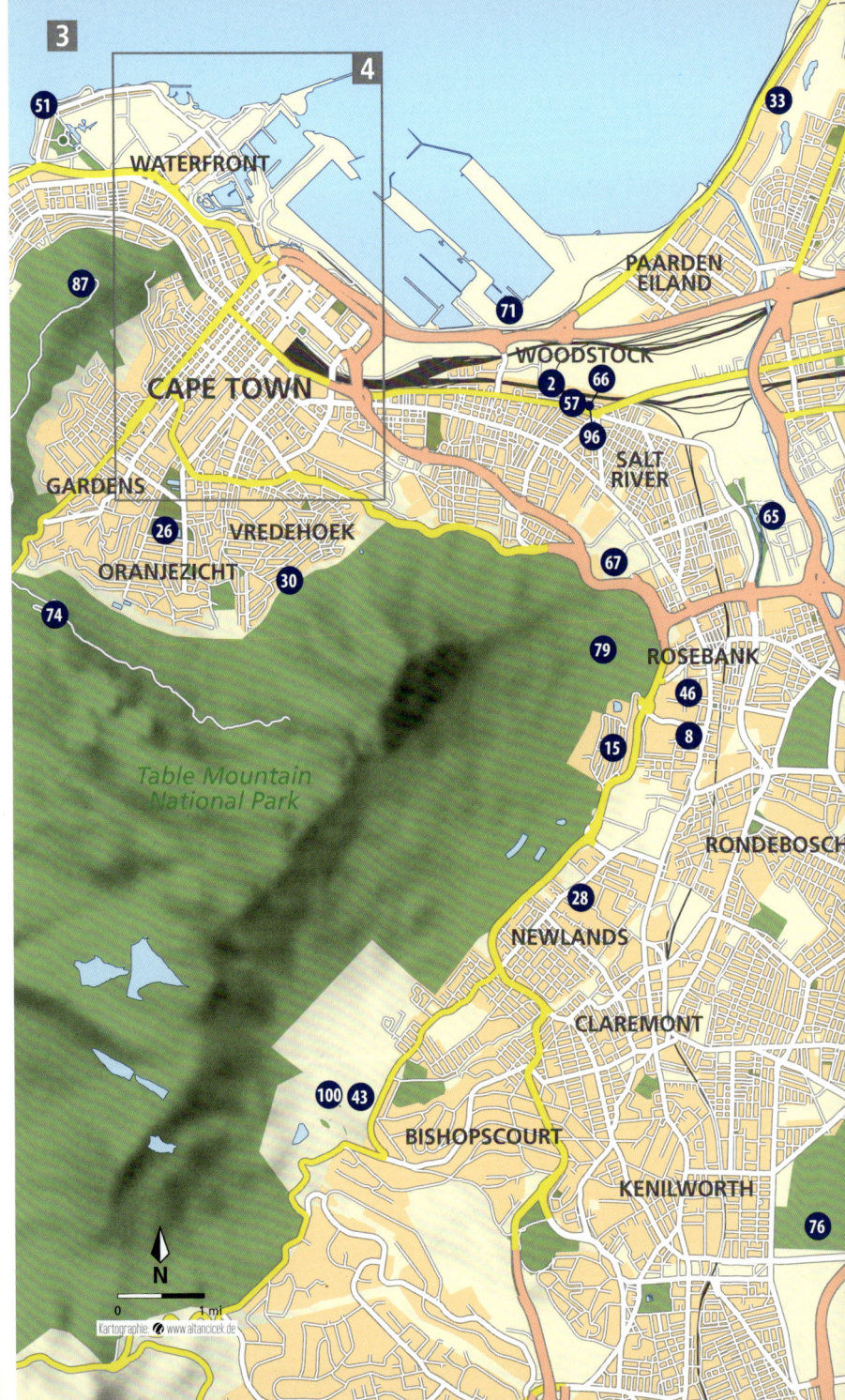

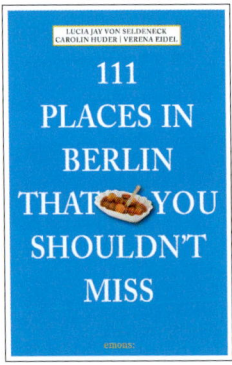

Lucia Jay von Seldeneck,
Carolin Huder, Verena Eidel
**111 PLACES IN BERLIN
THAT YOU SHOULDN'T MISS**
ISBN 978-3-95451-208-9

Rüdiger Liedtke
**111 PLACES IN MUNICH
THAT YOU SHOULDN'T MISS**
ISBN 978-3-95451-222-5

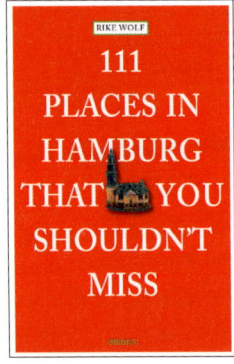

Rike Wolf
**111 PLACES IN HAMBURG
THAT YOU SHOULDN'T MISS**
ISBN 978-3-95451-234-8

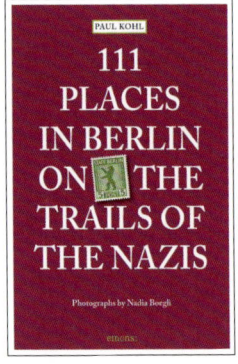

Paul Kohl
**111 PLACES IN BERLIN
ON THE TRAIL OF THE NAZIS**
ISBN 978-3-95451-323-9

John Sykes
**111 PLACES IN LONDON
THAT YOU SHOULDN'T MISS**
ISBN 978-3-95451-346-8

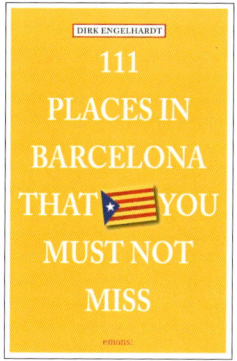

Dirk Engelhardt
**111 PLACES IN BARCELONA
THAT YOU MUST NOT MISS**
ISBN 978-3-95451-353-6

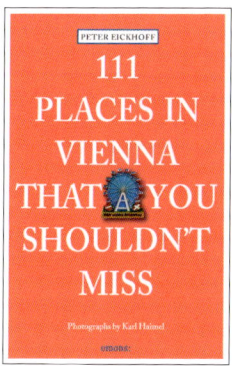

Peter Eickhoff
**111 PLACES IN VIENNA
THAT YOU SHOULDN'T MISS**
ISBN 978-3-95451-206-5

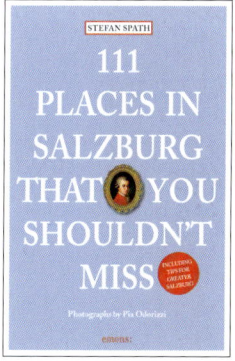

Stefan Spath
**111 PLACES IN SALZBURG
THAT YOU SHOULDN'T MISS**
ISBN 978-3-95451-230-0

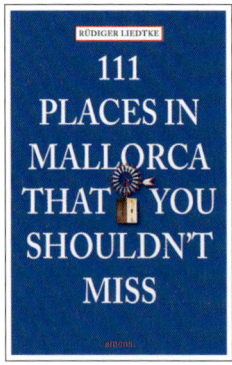

Rüdiger Liedtke
**111 PLACES ON MALLORCA
THAT YOU SHOULDN'T MISS**
ISBN 978-3-95451-281-2

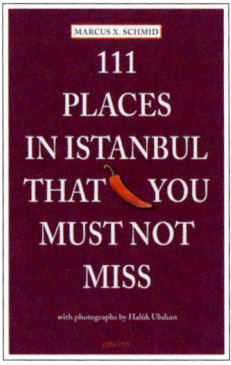

Marcus X. Schmid
**111 PLACES IN ISTANBUL
THAT YOU MUST NOT MISS**
ISBN 978-3-95451-423-6

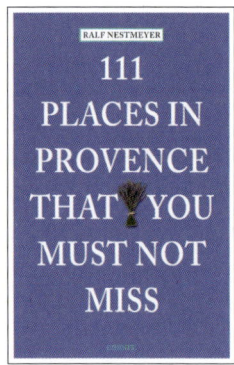

Ralf Nestmeyer
**111 PLACES IN PROVENCE
THAT YOU MUST NOT MISS**
ISBN 978-3-95451-422-9

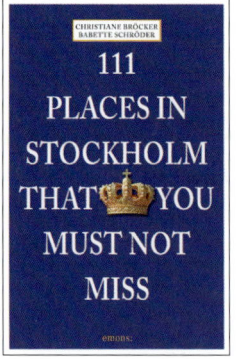

Christiane Bröcker,
Babette Schröder
**111 PLACES IN STOCKHOLM
THAT YOU MUST NOT MISS**
ISBN 978-3-95451-459-5

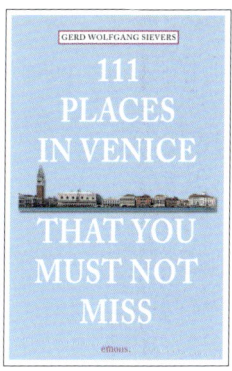

Gerd Wolfgang Sievers
111 PLACES IN VENICE THAT YOU MUST NOT MISS
ISBN 978-3-95451-460-1

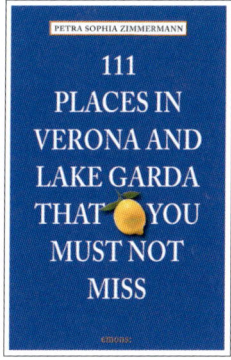

Petra Sophia Zimmermann
111 PLACES IN VERONA AND LAKE GARDA THAT YOU MUST NOT MISS
ISBN 978-3-95451-611-7

Annett Klingner
111 PLACES IN ROME THAT YOU MUST NOT MISS
ISBN 978-3-95451-469-4

Jo-Anne Elikann
111 PLACES IN NEW YORK THAT YOU MUST NOT MISS
ISBN 978-3-95451-052-8

Photo credits:
All photos © Rüdiger Liedtke and © Laszlo Trankovits,
except chapter 42 (iStockphoto.com /DanComaniciu), 30 (Markus Schönherr), 4 (Picture:ParliamentofRSA), 93 (Kirstin Palitza).

Photos © Rüdiger Liedtke for the chapters: 1, 3, 5, 6, 9, 10, 12, 13, 16, 19, 20, 21, 22, 23, 25, 26, 29, 31, 34, 40, 44, 45, 47, 50, 51, 53, 54, 58, 60, 61, 62, 63, 64, 66, 67, 68, 69, 71, 72, 75, 78, 79, 80, 81, 82, 83, 86, 87, 88, 90, 91, 92, 94, 95, 96, 97, 101, 104, 105, 106, 110

Photos © Laszlo Trankovits for the chapters: 2, 7, 8, 11, 14, 15, 17, 18, 24, 27, 28, 32, 33, 35, 36, 37, 38, 39, 41, 43, 46, 48, 49, 52, 55, 56, 57, 59, 65, 70, 73, 74, 76, 77, 84, 85, 89, 98, 99, 100, 102, 103, 107, 108, 109, 111

Special thanks to Susanne Schubert. Thanks also to Klaus Neumann, Kristin Palitza and Markus Schönherr.

Rüdiger Liedtke, author and journalist, has written four other books in the 111 series about Munich and Mallorca.

Laszlo Trankovits, journalist and author, worked as a correspondent and head of the African section of the German Press Agency in Cape Town until 2014.